Lost Under the Lion's Shadow

David Ray

Lost Under the Lion's Shadow
by David Ray

Printed in the United States of America

ISBN 9781628390070

Unless otherwise indicated, Bible quotations are taken from the New International Version. Copyright © 1984 by Cambridge University Press.

www.xulonpress.com

Something has gone wrong with the human race, and we know it. Better said, something has gone wrong **within** the human race. It doesn't take a theologian or a psychologist to tell you that. Read a newspaper. Spend a weekend with your relatives. Pay attention to the movements of your own heart in a single day. Most of the misery we suffer on this planet is the fruit of the human heart gone bad. This glorious treasure has been stained, marred, infected. Sin enters the story and spreads like a computer virus.

John Eldredge, <u>Epic</u>

Prologue

The water was higher than I had anticipated. It had been raining all week at camp, but the roar of the normally undersized stream was still surprising. When I had waded across earlier in the week, the water barely reached my shins, but now the chocolate-colored mix was considerably deeper and definitely more powerful. The options were simple; the choice was not. I could wait it out or try to cross. With the showers continuing, there was no guarantee as to how long I might have to delay. My scheduled plans to get out of the wilderness would certainly have to be postponed. It wouldn't be the end of the world, but it would be inconvenient for those who were counting on my timely return.

I was already soaking wet from the rain. If I fell in and took a dousing, I couldn't get much wetter than I already was, so I decided to press forward. I was ready to get off of the muddy trail and get home. Unsnapping my pack's padded waist belt, I took the first step into the raging torrent. The water only came up to mid-thigh, but it was extremely strong. I was careful with each step, making sure to brace my boot before seeking to move to the next foothold. My hiking staff was an important third leg. Carrying a heavy pack always made footing treacherous, but with the water so murky, I was only able to continue making progress by feeling for each step. However, with each stride I felt increasingly more comfortable.

It probably wasn't the safest of decisions, but I was going to survive the crossing. Once across, there still remained a half-day's hike, but I was going to get back to the truck in time to complete my plans. With barely 15 feet remaining, the water was getting shallower. Another few steps would have me on the rocks and to safety. I thought about what I might have for supper after getting cleaned up and warm, but suddenly the rock I was bracing my boot against began to roll in the current. Frantic, I attempted to find another firm foothold, but it was as if all the rocks were moving underneath the rolling flood. I was going to get even wetter. I dropped to my knees, thinking that I could crawl out the last few feet, but it didn't play out that way. The powerful water grabbed me and immediately twisted me upside down.

I scrambled to disengage the pack from my shoulders, but the force of the water pinned me against it. With the pack still strapped on, I was moving downstream at an extraordinary speed. Still battling to slip free from the pack straps, the wild water sucked me under. The muddy mixture closed in over my face. My world grew dark. I could do nothing except relax and give myself over to the inevitable.

CHAPTER 1

Desire to Disappear

The plane was descending, readying for final approach. The adjustment in cabin pressure aroused me from my nap. It took me a moment to regain my bearings and recognize that it had only been a dream, perhaps more accurately a nightmare, one of many over the last several months. My heart was still pounding against my chest. Sliding open the port window, I peered into the ragged belly of the snow capped southern Andes. I was ready to be disengaged, and not just from the cramped airline seat. The struggles of the last year had truly abused my heart.

Stretching my legs under the seat allowed the feeling of life to return as the blood began to recirculate. It was only moments later before I could sense the familiar grind of the landing gear lowering. As the plane banked sharply, I caught a glimpse of the city of Bariloche nestled in its mountain basin. I scarcely had time to remove my earplugs before the wheels skipped once and the jets reversed power, bringing the *Aerolineas Argentinas* to taxi speed. As the Airbus cornered on the taxiway, I had my first view of San Carlos de Bariloche International Airport.

The city of Bariloche is set in the midst of the majestic Andes along the perimeter of the Seven Sister Lakes, and from the plane appeared to be much larger than I had anticipated. However, the landscape opposite from the city and mountains, which was my destination, revealed complete desolation. That's exactly what I was hoping. Across the Pampas there was scarcely any sign of life; not a tree, not a structure, just an open sea of endless prairie grass.

I have always loved people, but at least for the current season, I wasn't in the mindset to be with anyone. As the plane waited on the tarmac, I reconsidered why I was in Argentina. I simply wanted to disappear. I was exhausted trying to explain all that had happened in and around my life. Rachel and I had been married for nearly twenty-four years. They had been wonderful years until those last several months. The Rachel I had known simply vanished. One evening we were laughing and relaxing together; the next morning the smile had been wiped clean. It never returned.

Anger and bitterness moved into our home and took over like an arctic storm. At first I tried to understand what had created the metamorphosis, and then a feeble attempt to remedy, but I was unsuccessful in both. Nothing made any sense. She had always been proud of me as her husband. She was pleased that I served as a pastor in a wonderful Christian congregation. She enjoyed hearing me preach week after week, and was delighted even more knowing that most of the congregation loved and respected me. That all changed over night without explanation.

I attempted to keep a cover on my own fears and my wife's tragic shift in attitude. The consistent need to offer excuses and apologies, coupled with juggling my own undefined guilt, real or imagined, consumed most of my available energy. After surviving seven months of this living hell, I concluded that for the good of all, I needed to step down as pastor. There were absolutely no other plans on my agenda. I simply did what I felt that I had to do.

The reality is that some of my closest friends had recommended such a step, but I had agreed with them. Two weeks after I had officially "retired," the doctors discovered the tumor in my wife's frontal lobe. Many of my questions were immediately answered; many more were raised. Three months later, her funeral closed that chapter in my life. The entire tragedy wounded me deeply. We had many friends, or at least we did before Rachel's illness. In that last year most of our relationships had grown strained. Rachel had begun to fabricate lies, many of them about me. Few really believed her fantasy tales, but it cast a shadow over all of our lives and relationships. None of us had a clue concerning her sickness.

Her transformation was so violent that it bred insecurity within my own spirit. I didn't know what to say, and most of our friends didn't know how to respond. Once the cancer was discovered, the progression was rapid. We spent most of the next three months out of town seeking treatment from the best doctors, and away from our friends. After her death, the majority of our friends resumed their own busy lives. Without my wife and without my career, I felt like I no longer belonged anywhere, and to be honest, it was more than a feeling.

Both of our daughters were deeply concerned and attempted to reach out. They wanted to help, but what could they do? Both had finished their educations and were busy beginning their own families. I was extremely proud of both daughters and my sons-in-law, but none of them had fully realized the extent of their mom's condition before or after the discovery of her disease. I loved them with all my heart, but at least in my mind, I would have been imposing to accept their requests to come and stay. I needed some other alternative.

Truthfully, I felt like my prior life was in some way completed, and it was time to explore what the future might hold. I could almost taste the sweetness of a new adventure, but I would never have publicly voiced such sentiments. Such thoughts seemed so uncaring and inappropriate. I could barely admit to myself that feelings like those were wandering around in my heart. Over the years as a pastor, I had helped more than a few work through their personal losses, but I had never realized how confusing grief could be. One moment my heart would be so heavy that I wasn't certain that I could even breathe, but then, like flipping a light switch, the excitement of starting over would put a gleam in my eyes and a skip in my step. I didn't understand either emotion, and perhaps that's the major reason for the desire to disappear for at least a week on an Argentinean trout stream.

With the house empty and a light spring snow falling, I searched the Internet one afternoon and placed a phone call. There was nothing on my calendar. After removing the recurring duties and responsibilities that had been my life as a pastor for years, there was literally nothing on my smartphone calendar except a few birthday reminders. There was no reason for me not to spend some time doing something else, being somewhere else and perhaps even becoming someone else. Why not go fishing? I had never had the time nor finances for such an adventure, but now neither were a difficulty. I was on my way to South America scarcely six days after the initial search on the Internet.

The fishing lodge and guide service I located had emphasized on their web page that their clients could fish as hard and as long as they desired. Their exclusive fishing lodge, the Rojas Pampas Estancia, only entertained four fishermen at a time. Scanning their promotional blurb made it sound exactly what I needed, or at least what I thought I needed. Once I retrieved my bag and had my passport stamped, I stepped out into the fresh mountain air. A handful of taxis and shuttle vans were standing nearby. Without having to look, I found Ramon holding a cardboard sign with "Richard Dempsey" hastily scrawled with a green marker. That was me. Within minutes we were bouncing past the edge of what appeared to be a village directly from the Swiss Alps toward the remote fishing lodge in the Patagonia region. With every bounce I felt the pressure of last year lift. The road hugged the base of the mountains, and I simply relaxed as the beauty of the stark and rugged landscape unfolded before me.

We arrived at the Rojas Pampas Lodge after the sun had already dropped behind the impressive westward peaks. Supper was waiting for me, though the others had previously eaten. Two of the other clients were relaxing in front of the massive stone fireplace with their favorite drinks. They were friendly Texans who were excited about the next morning's fishing adventure. They had been on other guided fishing trips together, but Patagonia was one of their particular dreams, and they had been preparing and planning for this trip for some time.

Nothing was said about the third client, assuming that I was the fourth. However, after the flights from Lexington to Dallas, then Buenos Aires, and finally Bariloche, followed by nearly four hours in the shuttle van, I was exhausted and ready to find my bed even with the three-hour time change. With its knotty pine paneling, slanted ceiling and rustic furnishings, my room had a warm and comfortable feel, but that mattered little in my condition. I scarcely even noticed the large painting over the bed reflecting the powerful face of an impressive African lion. In the king-sized sturdy bed, I drifted into the dream world of no return. It felt wonderful to have disappeared.

CHAPTER 2

Flash of Color

Without an alarm, I roused at my usual 5:30 AM. I normally read, journaled and prayed in the mornings, but of late my normal routines had become nonexistent. It wasn't that I had grown lazy, but that my spirit was exhausted. I didn't have anything to say, and I wasn't certain that God did either, at least to me.

I had been a man of faith since my teenage years, but this past year had rocked me internally. I wasn't ready to confess it, but I wasn't sure what I really believed anymore. As a career pastor, I would have had to work through those feelings of doubt before delivering a message on Sunday, but now I was facing a whole new world without weekly deadlines. I felt no time pressure to deal with such a crisis in faith. I realized that I was no longer being paid to "believe." It concerned me to admit that, but in another way it felt honest and real. It didn't even enter my mind that this was Sunday morning.

Quickly unpacking the remainder of my gear and lacing my boots, I stepped into the crisp early morning. Before the others were stirring, I walked down from the lodge towards the river. I could hear the tumble of the falling waters before I could see. Remembering what I had read in the promotional material, I was realizing why they recommended various levels of warm clothing. I could see my own breath, as the eastern sky gradually grew lighter. A wisp of high clouds began to reflect the hint of the bright morning colors. It felt right to breathe in the beauty of this amazing panorama.

When I returned to the lodge, breakfast was being served. The Rojases owned the exclusive fishing lodge, and worked the extensive sheep and cattle ranch, but they were on vacation. Mexico City shopping is what I think I had overheard. In their stead, Morena was the host, cook and housekeeper. She wore a big smile and bright yellow cotton dress, but apparently didn't speak much English. The two Texans, Ben and Robert, had just served themselves from the skillets and Dutch ovens on the counter. There was a woman already seated at the guest table. After I found the eggs, and a variety of sausages and sweet breads, I joined the threesome.

Her name was Rebekah. She said she was from Boston. She seemed pleasant, but as she politely spoke with the Texans, I realized that it had never entered my mind that the four fishing clients at the Rojas's lodge might not all be male. I also concluded that with the two Texans planning their full day together, that I was looking across the table at my fishing partner for the day, and probably for the entire week. The thought of that prospect was weird, to be truthful, but the more I continued glancing across the rustic oak table, the more I warmed to the idea. Her blue and black flannel shirt accented her blue eyes.

Noticing a wedding ring, I was curious why she was on a trip like this by herself if she was married. I didn't feel comfortable pursuing her story during breakfast in the presence of the others; that would need to wait. It was evident that we would have time together as the day and week progressed. Before we had finished our very tasty and ample breakfast, our fishing guides made their entrance. They grabbed plates of victuals and mugs of hot brew and joined our table. The conversation immediately turned to the fishing plans for the day. The two guides filled the room with energy.

Santiago seemed to have fished around the world, having finally settled here on the Patagonia region. His face reflected experience, character and warmth. His bold laughter lighted the room. Mateo was much younger. He had grown up in the area and had fished the rivers of Patagonia all his life. It was decided that Mateo would be guiding the Texans downstream. Tales of last week's hatch and resulting battles were repeated with great gusto. Santiago would be leading Rebekah and myself upstream. After a brief exhortation concerning what to bring with us, we busied ourselves preparing for the day's adventure.

With our gear stored on board, we both climbed into the back seat of a well-used Toyota Land Cruiser. Our guide had the front passenger seat full of additional fishing gear, a small ice chest, bottles of water and a cardboard box stuffed with various food items. Santiago seemed to be focused upon Rebekah in the back seat as we headed west towards the mountains. It was clear that he didn't guide many unaccompanied women, and he was obviously trying to assess her fishing experience, if not other aspects as well.

She didn't seem to mind answering his multiple questions, though she answered without any elaborations. She didn't speak with much of an accent, but it was clear that she was from the East Coast. As we arrived at our day's destination, I realized that I had spoken scarcely a word to either Santiago or Rebekah on the short trip, though my eyes more than occasionally wandered in her direction. As she and Santiago continued their conversation about the Patagonia area, it registered with me that I was a single man. It had been almost six months, but the realization that I was no longer married had not fully settled into my heart. I also noticed that I was still wearing my wedding band.

It didn't take long to hoist on the waders, assemble our fly rods and tie on Santiago's recommended fly pattern. It was a variant of a grasshopper trailed by a small black midge. The river appeared to be like any number of streams in the West that I had fished many times before, and I felt comfortable. On the third cast I netted a fat 15-inch rainbow trout after a feisty run. Rebekah and Santiago were a hundred yards upstream. It appeared that she needed more special attention from Santiago than I did.

After landing a dozen or more healthy fish, Santiago walked down and joined me, suggesting a different fly pattern. I was content with my current selection, but I submitted to his wisdom. On the second drift through a deep cut, a monster rose and flicked at my offering. The fish repeated on the next cast, taking the dropper fly, but this time the battle was on. The power of this fish was impressive. This is why folks travel to the tip of the world just to toss a tiny imitation insect.

It took about ten minutes before the brute finally decided to yield and turn on her side. Having rolled multiple times and jumping completely out of the water at least five, the big brown finally slipped into Santiago's landing net. I realized then why he carried such a large mouthed net. After a quick photo opportunity, the twelve-pound beauty was released to again haunt the depths. It was then that I noticed that Rebekah had been watching the battle from the top of the bank behind me. She waved my direction in celebration.

Santiago suggested that Rebekah should try the hole just above where I had landed my trophy. I decided that I needed to show the same professional courtesy, and watch her fishing skills as she had mine. She had already landed several handsome trout with Santiago at her side, so she was confident. The guide sat down beside me so that he, too, could observe her fishing abilities. Santiago and I didn't have much to say to each other as we watched her delicately and skillfully present her fly over the deep run.

In less than five minutes, another mighty brown showed himself violently attacking her fly presentation. Santiago hurried down to join her with his net, but the line snapped before he could offer help. She just cackled with joy as the adrenaline coursed through her veins. If my line had snapped on my monster, I would have been disappointed, and maybe angry, but she was laughing. As I yelled a word of encouragement towards her, I admitted to myself that I was beginning to enjoy her presence. I wanted to find out what made her tick inside. What was her story?

Santiago suggested that Rebekah and I should fish the next hole together while he prepared lunch. We both landed some very healthy fish, but no giants flashed up from the deep. Eventually we joined him on the bank overlooking the stream. He presented a tasty lunch on a small table for two covered with a red checked tablecloth. We started with a cup of hot bean soup, and then helped ourselves to a variety of finger foods, some of Morena's specialties no doubt. With Rebekah still giggling and the massive mountains as our backdrop, I had to confess to myself that this was fun. The laughter, the warmth and pure joy of the day's fishing made the last year seem increasingly like a distant memory.

With Santiago cleaning up from the meal, I decided it was time to ask the obvious, "I'm curious. Why did you decide to come on a fishing trip to Argentina alone?"

She responded, still with laughter not far from her face, "It just seemed like the thing to do. Gary and I talked about coming down to Patagonia to fish so many times, but we never did."

"Who is Gary?" I asked probably knowing the answer.

"My husband," she said.

"Why didn't he come with you?" I continued.

She replied, "Why didn't your wife come with you?" She pointed towards my wedding band. The laughter seemed to be evaporating. The change in her mood caught me off guard. I didn't want to spoil the season, so we sat in silence for a few uncomfortable moments. Finally I explained to her, "I lost my wife last year. Cancer is brutal." I had no desire to offer any more explanation, and she didn't ask.

Her voice was softer as she looked into my eyes and said, "Oh, I'm sorry. I saw your wedding band."

I nodded, but didn't respond. A black-chested eagle flew directly over us watching our every move. We didn't speak as we observed the powerful bird lazily float off into the distance towards the rugged mountain peaks.

"I've lost my husband, too," she said almost in a matter-of-fact manner. I waited for her to continue not sure how to respond. Eventually she added, "His brother tricked him into a business deal that apparently involved them with some shady characters from Mexico. By the time Gary figured out that it was going sour, it was too late. He and his brother left for a business trip and never came home."

The sun felt good on our shoulders. I didn't ask any more questions, and I wasn't sure she wanted to offer any further details.

"The FBI told me, after a year's investigation, that they believed that both of the brothers had been killed, probably in Mexico. No bodies were discovered. It's been four years now. I've moved on."

"That's horrible," I said, half under my breath. My words sounded trite and shallow, but it was clear that Rebekah had nothing more to say about her husband.

We continued to sip our hot *mate* herbal tea, a new and pleasant experience for both of us. The warm noon sun felt good on our shoulders. Neither of us knew what else to say. We fished the rest of the afternoon sharing the holes together. Each fish caught was held so that the other could see and admire. A few pictures were taken. Santiago was always near, but neither of us paid him much attention. His expansive landing net wasn't needed again, but that didn't seem to matter much to either of us. We fished, laughed and completely enjoyed the day, and each other, mostly without words.

Morena and the Lodge put on a magnificent show for dinner after the first full day of fishing. Perfectly grilled bone-in rib-eye steaks topped off the menu. The cuts were seasoned with a unique rub and were so tender they could be cut with a fork. We savored every morsel. The laughing resumed for all of us. Ben and Robert caught more fish than Rebekah and I, but their quantity didn't compare to the quality of my one trophy. In jest, they decided that they should go with Santiago tomorrow instead of Mateo. After considerable halfhearted negotiations, they decided that it was probably Rebekah that created my good luck, and determined that she should go with them instead, but that I could keep Santiago.

Rebekah shut down their good-natured humor, saying with a slight wink, "You can have Santiago, but I think I'll keep Richard." The Texans laughed and cat-called, but to be honest from my perspective, her words felt pleasing to hear.

It was getting late and we needed to get our sleep, but silently I stepped out onto the front porch. The temperature had already dropped and it was crisp. The full moon lit up the wide-open prairie. It had been a wonderful and a surprising day, but it was too cold to stay outside for long. While it was towards the end of winter back in Kentucky, it was the beginning of fall here on the steppes of Patagonia. As I turned to go inside, I saw the rustic wooden door open. Rebekah stepped out onto the porch and joined me.

"I was wondering where you disappeared to," she said from the darkness of the porch.

"I just love the night air, especially with the full moon. Always have," I said without looking back at her.

She didn't immediately respond. The air was getting even colder. A brisk breeze was slipping down from the mountains across the Pampas bringing more than a hint of frost.

"I enjoyed today," she said with her teeth beginning to chatter, and her arms wrapped around herself.

"So did I, but it's cold out here. We better go back inside," I said with some reluctance.

Back in the warmth, we stood a moment together before the fireplace allowing the soft glow of the coals to rediscover our backsides. Without another word, we each found our separate rooms. I was feeling something deep inside that I hadn't felt in a long time. I think she was, too. In any case, I looked forward to the morning.

CHAPTER 3

Empty House

The next day was almost a repeat to the previous. The weather was amazing, with the sky so deeply blue that it seemed to beg just to be admired. The fish, however, apparently were taking the day off. Rebekah and I caught more than our share, and we certainly weren't disappointed, but the giant trophy trout didn't seem to be interested and wouldn't move. Santiago had taken us to a different river closer to the mountain peaks. It was a smaller stream and felt somewhat colder through the waders, but it was so clear that the gravel bottom appeared, as if being seen through fine crystal.

Our streamside lunch with Santiago was again superb. A variety of meat and cheese *empanadas* were very tasty, followed by croissants covered with a local bilberry jam; it reminded us that Argentina was widely known for its love of great food. It was as if Rebekah and I had become old friends. Neither of us talked about our pasts, or even our families, and yet we both continued sharing, as we felt more and more comfortable. Being from Boston, such openness and trust didn't come natural for Rebekah, but slowly she opened her heart and shared.

Once we completed our leisurely lunch, we finally turned back to consider the river. As we started the climb down to the water, I held out my hand to help Rebekah negotiate the steep rocky slide. She didn't hesitate to accept my offering. Once she negotiated the climb in her waders, we released hands. We both sensed that we needed to be careful. Both of our hearts had been deeply wounded, and neither of us was ready to become vulnerable again. We enjoyed each other too much that we didn't dare do anything to spoil the moment, or make it complicated.

Part of me wasn't sure that I would ever be ready for another relationship. The pain of that last year of marriage had marked me. I wasn't certain who I was anymore. However, I found myself glancing Rebekah's direction over and over. She was beautiful, but not so much as Hollywood defined beauty. She had poise, grace and perhaps even a hint of majesty as she moved, even in her waders. Her skin seemed to reflect the quality of the clear running streams. With her sandy blond hair tucked under her fishing cap, and her blue eyes mirroring the sky, she looked amazing. I definitely wasn't ready to admit anything even to myself, but I was certainly more than interested.

As we were breaking down our gear for the ride back to Rojas Estancia, I noticed a cloud of dust in the distance. It seemed to be coming our direction, working its way along the winding stream. As we continued loading the equipment, I realized that since leaving the Lodge yesterday morning, we had not seen one vehicle, or even another human being. This tributary of the Rio Traful had been only for us. The sight of the oncoming jeep reminded me that there were other people in this world, and probably this intruder had as much right to be here as we did. It dawned on me that I hadn't even thought about anyone else, at least over the last couple of days, unless of course I counted Rebekah.

Santiago obviously recognized the jeep and its occupants. With a flurry of dust, they pulled up beside our Land Cruiser. Santiago was all smiles as he introduced us to Alfonzo and his fishing client, Danny from southern California. Alfonso guided for a lodge several miles to the North, Santiago explained; they had been fishing on the river where we had fished yesterday. Danny had hooked at least two true trophies, but neither fish were brought to the landing net. His face was still flushed with the excitement as he tried to explain how the fish outsmarted and outmuscled him.

Alfonso probed us for our fishing report, and we obliged. He assumed, as anyone might, that Rebekah and I were a couple, and naturally referenced that observation in his questions. We quickly corrected him, but I wasn't certain that he believed us by the look on his face. He asked us the typical questions, including where we were from and how long we planned to stay. Upon hearing that Rebekah was from Boston, he quipped, "I once guided for a gentleman from Boston, but I haven't heard from him in over a year. I think his name was Gary, but I can't remember his last name. Perhaps you know a Gary from Boston that has fished down here?"

I could feel Rebekah tighten up. It was an uncomfortable moment for her, but the other guide didn't pick up on it. Finally Rebekah snapped, "Big city," and the conversation screeched to a halt. Her response didn't invite additional questions.

Alfonso, sensing what appeared to be unfriendliness, said, "*Señora*, I'm glad that you came to our proud country. I trust that our trout will spoil you so that you will return many times. Santiago is a good friend, and experienced fishing guide, and the Rojas Pampas is a wonderful lodge. Santiago will put you over some great Patagonian fish. *Buenas tardes*, and good luck."

With that, Alfonso and Danny were gone in a cloud of dust. As Santiago backed up the Land Cruiser, he leaned over the seat and said, "Alfonso has never even been to Buenos Aires, much less to Boston. He just assumed that you would know everybody in Boston like he knows everybody in his village."

In a subtle way, Santiago was defending his fellow fishing guide while rebuking Rebekah's apparent unfriendliness. She caught his message, but didn't immediately respond. As we drove towards the Lodge for the evening, we hardly spoke. The sunset had the entire sky on fire, silhouetting the magnificent Andes. There was little more to be said. However, with the Lodge in sight, Rebekah said with an air of confession, "I used to be married to a Gary, and we always talked about coming down here but we never made it. He was killed several years ago, so I decided that I would come alone, perhaps to honor his memory." Neither Santiago nor I responded.

The rest of the week unfolded as if a world-renowned artist had scripted it. Each river held fish, beautiful fish and powerful fish. We both landed several true Argentinean trophies, but we had many more break off after screaming out the line. Rainbows, browns and some brilliantly colored brookies were the order for each day. The weather was glorious, the food was spectacular, and the companionship was astonishing. Each evening Rebekah and I would walk from the Rojas Lodge along the river, and just recap the day's experience together. Again, little was said about our pasts, but much was said about our hopes and dreams.

Strangely, I never mentioned that just nine months before I had been a pastor. She hadn't asked and I hadn't volunteered that information, but I hadn't asked her what she did back in Boston either. We both acted like those chapters in our lives were not as important as the experiences of today. We knew our fellow guests, the two Texas friends, assumed that after our long evening private walks along the river, that one of us was sneaking into the other's bedroom, but such wasn't the case. It wouldn't have been right, though I must admit the thought did flutter through my mind once or twice.

On Sunday morning the shuttle van was coming to transport us back to the Bariloche airport. The Texans were staying one more night, so as we said our good byes and loaded our bags, they headed out to fish another day. We both envied them. Neither one of us was ready for this magical week to end, but the shuttle van headed north nevertheless. As we bounced on the back roads, we retold the stories of the fish. It seemed that the big ones that escaped were more embellished in our memories than the ones we eased into our landing nets. I hoped that pattern wouldn't continue in our relationship. A brilliant rainbow in the Western sky bid us farewell to Patagonia.

My flight was to take me back to Buenos Aires, and then to Dallas, and then home to Lexington in the heart of the Blue Grass State. Rebekah's flight was leaving an hour after mine, but it was taking her over the mountains to Santiago, Chili, then on to Miami before ending up in Boston.

A few minutes before I was to board, I finally asked, "May I call you?" After this amazing week, it seemed like such a silly thing to request. I felt embarrassed, but I also felt almost desperate. I had no way to contact her, and such a thought almost made me queasy. With a faint smile, she moved in close and gently kissed me. I kissed her back as the intercom announced the boarding of my flight.

She handed me her business card: *Rebekah Black, Upscale Furniture and Fine Décor*, followed by a Boston address and telephone. Then she said in my ear, "My personal number is on the back." Her eyes warned me that I better call.

I wanted to give her my card as well, but all I had were some old church business cards. They were out of date, and I didn't want to do any explaining. We hugged again before I moved towards the door to board. Inside me was the strangest mixture of emotions. Part of me wanted to jump with joy, but another part of me wanted to turnaround and stay forever. As I entered the plane, a painful question jumped out at me: *To what and whom was I going home to?*

With my seat belt snug, the plane pulled away. In a few moments it was banking away from the majestic Andes and climbing toward Buenos Aires. I clutched Rebekah's business card in my front pocket, buttoning it up for safekeeping. It had been an exhilarating week, a life-renewing week.

CHAPTER 4

Secrets

The flights were uneventful except the obnoxious drunk on the leg to Dallas. He had a few drinks served by the flight attendant, but it appeared he had spent some time in the bar before boarding. By the time we were touching down, I was tired of listening to his loud and vulgar nonsense. He didn't make Texas proud. I was secretly hoping that he would be transferring on to Oklahoma or Arkansas, but he was probably from Dallas. Having been raised in Texas myself, I found myself defending the Lone Star State, though I had lived in Kentucky the last twenty years.

Home was as quiet as I feared. After checking the mail, calling my daughters, paying a few bills online, watering the houseplants and standing forever under a hot shower, I wanted to call Boston, but she wouldn't be home yet. While checking the refrigerator and finding absolutely nothing edible, I realized that such was my new life: a big lonely house and a forever empty refrigerator. I tossed out a couple of unidentifiable leftovers. There weren't but a few messages on the answering machine. That didn't surprise me, because I never answered the home phone anyway, but it was pleasing to know that the candidate for the governor of Kentucky was highly interested in my vote.

In the past I would have turned on the television and surfed the news and sports until I couldn't fight off sleep any longer, but tonight I just sat in my leather easy chair and stared at the blank screen. Perhaps Rebekah would be home shortly. I read her card again, studying each letter and number, tracing each with my finger. Finally, I decided to text her. If she responded to the text, then I would call. I felt like a junior high kid inviting a girl to the big dance. The text message was simple, "Have you made it home safe?" She didn't respond.

On Monday morning there was still no response to my text. My thoughts bounced between the far limits of my imagination, but I tried my best to hold the reins to my fears. I had some personal business to run down through the morning—the bank, pharmacy, grocery, dry cleaners, and I even stopped by to check in at Hope Fellowship, my previous congregation. Other than a sack of junk mail with my name on the address, there was little for me to do at Hope. My office had been transformed into a workroom for the children's ministry. Things seemed to be going very smoothly without me. My old secretary asked about my fishing trip, but it was obvious that she didn't have much time to visit. Life at Hope was full and busy, just as my life was empty and quiet. There was still no response from the text.

As I passed through the drive thru at Five Guys Burgers and Fries, my phone rang. It was an out of state number, but it wasn't either of the numbers from her business card. I knew it had to be from Boston with the "617" area code, but I didn't want to talk while trying to get my hamburger and fry order. I would call back immediately when I got home and could concentrate. Such a call was too important to risk while driving in traffic.

Sitting in the driveway with the Five Guys order being ignored, I checked the number against her card. It almost matched the handwritten private number she had written on the back of her business card. In her business, she must have multiple numbers. My heart was pounding. I punched the redial on the smartphone. The number started ringing, but I feared that it would be her secretary or business partner. When she answered, it didn't sound right. At first I was afraid that it was the wrong number. In any case this voice wasn't Rebekah's, so I asked if Rebekah was there. There was a long pause.

"Can we talk?" the weak voice said in a low tone.

Still confused I asked, "Rebekah, is that you?"

"Yes, but I need to talk to you. Can you come to Boston?" she asked.

Confused I responded, "Can you tell me what's happened?"

"I really want to talk face to face. I need to talk. I've found something that I need to show you," she continued in her muffled tone. I realized that she had been crying, at least I thought. It was hard to be certain over the phone. What had happened? What had changed

33

from yesterday morning at the airport? What did she need to show me? Without really thinking through everything, I knew that my calendar was still empty. There was no reason that I couldn't fly to Boston first thing in the morning. I told her that I would get a flight, and would let her know when I was to arrive. I thought I would have been excited, but something deep inside worried me. Something was desperately wrong. She was in trouble of some kind. Why couldn't she tell me over the phone?

My spirit was on high alert as I walked down the walkway at Boston's Logan. What was I walking into? At first I didn't even see her, but finally I noticed her standing back behind the crowd of usual greeters. She was waving, but without much enthusiasm dressed in all black. My heart was sinking. Something within was screaming to me that the glory of last week was being shattered like fine crystal right before my eyes.

She gave me a hug and said, "I'm glad you came." I hugged her back, but didn't try to kiss her. She looked so different than she had just two days before. Her face looked tense and tired. Her eyes no longer reflected the blue sky of the Patagonian prairie. She suggested that we sit down, so we found a booth in one of the many high-priced airport concessions. Before I could order my usual Diet Dr. Pepper, she ordered for both of us club sodas with lime. The drink orders gave us the privilege of sitting at their table.

"Tell me what has happened," I began when the waitress was out of range.

She reached into her leather purse and pulled out a passport. She handed it to me.

"What's this?" I asked.

"Look at it," she demanded almost with anger. It appeared to be her husband's passport.

"I assume that it is Gary's," I said.

She nodded and pulled out another passport handing it to me as well. It, too, reflected that it was Gary's. He had two passports.

"Do you remember the fellow we met along the river while fishing, the guide from the other lodge?" she asked.

I nodded and said, "He and his client from California were the only other persons we saw during the whole week. I think that his name was Alfonso, if I remember correctly."

"Do you remember what he said about guiding for a man named Gary from Boston?"

I nodded again, not understanding what she was meaning, but said, "You said that you and Gary never made the trip; you just talked about going."

"Look at the second passport I gave you," she insisted.

There was nothing on the first several pages, but then there were a series of entrance and exit visa stamps. A close examination of the faint ink revealed that they were Argentinean.

"So your husband went to Argentina?" I said not realizing the full meaning of that observation.

"According to that passport, eleven trips over three years. I found that passport in a bank deposit box that I didn't even know existed. The key to the box was taped under Gary's desk chair in our home office. There was also a key to a Post Office Box at a UPS Store. He was clearly hiding both from me.

"When I got home Sunday night, I dumped my suitcase on the office floor to sort it all out. That's when I saw something hanging from the bottom of the rolling office chair," her voice was growing stronger, but her face still showed the tension.

I didn't know what to say.

She continued, "The Post Office Box had a letter from a bank saying that the deposit box had been paid automatically. The bank deposit box contained three items: that second passport, the checkbook for an account that I didn't know existed and a Beretta 9 mm. Gary always said that he hated hand guns."

I could sense that the grief Rebekah had been experiencing had resurrected itself into real anger. Her husband had been living a second life behind her back. She had every right to be upset, even if it had been four years ago.

"You told me that he was involved in some kind of business with his brother. What kind of business was it?" I probed.

"He always told me that they were buying toys and craft items from Mexico and Bolivia, but I never saw any of it. To be honest, I don't really know," she responded.

We sat there in silence for a few minutes. We both sipped on our club sodas without realizing it.

"There's something else," she added. I was afraid to ask. "I asked the banker about the checking account. At first he didn't want to reveal anything to me, but after reviewing Gary's death certificate he agreed. Again, it wasn't our regular bank and the banker didn't know me, but he seemed to remember Gary quite well. The account is still active," she said as her voice broke. A few quiet tears began to flow. The emotional weight of the recent discoveries was taxing her in every way.

Offering her a napkin from the table dispenser in place of a Kleenex, I asked seeking to be sensitive, "What do you mean 'still active'?"

"There's over two million dollars in the account. Gary and I never had that kind of money. There are still monthly withdrawals. Cashier checks are being automatically sent to a Post Office box. You'll never guess where; some small town in Argentina," she said answering her own question.

"Two million dollars? That's a healthy account balance. How much are the monthly checks?" I said trying to grasp the magnitude.

"Fifteen thousand every month and that's been happening for the last 4 years," she responded, "but there is no way to know who is cashing them, at least not from here. I need to go back to Argentina and find out. I don't want to go by myself; I want you to go with me. I need you to go."

Two days ago I never wanted to leave Patagonia. Yesterday I would have gone back on a whim. Now it all seemed surreal. The thought of being with Rebekah again was inviting; the thought of being with her under these conditions sent cold chills down my spine. As the waitress offered refills and left the bill, I checked my calendar mostly out of habit. There were still no meetings, counseling sessions, or sermon preparation time scheduled. The life of a modern pastor is on overload most of the time. Today my calendar was blank; as blank as the last time I checked.

There was no reason not to go back to Argentina. No matter how I felt, I could not have said, "No," any more than I could have jumped over the Grand Canyon. As I started to check on flights with my phone, Rebekah shook her head. She confessed that she had already confirmed two reservations leaving this Sunday, one from Boston, and another from Lexington. She knew that I would say yes, or at least was hoping; no, she knew. After all, here I was sitting with her in Boston without a moment's hesitation.

"What do you expect to find back in Argentina?" I asked realizing that I should have said, "We."

"I'm not sure," she said with a touch of last week's smile, "but I'm glad you're going with me. Thanks," and she took my hand. I thought about kissing her, but it didn't seem the time or place, sitting in the busy airport crowd, at least not the place.

CHAPTER 5

Shadows

It was a difficult wait until Sunday. Rebekah and I talked every evening and texted several times each day. She was convinced that we could just walk into the post office in the small Argentinean village and find out who was picking up the monthly checks. I wasn't so sure it would be that simple, but even if it were, what then? Who could it be? Who was collecting $15,000 monthly and had been for over four years, and why? Where did that money come from? What had Gary and his brother really been exporting? What happened to the two brothers? There were so many unanswered questions.

I suggested to Rebekah that perhaps she should call the FBI and involve them again, but she didn't think it was a good idea, at least not yet. What was she to tell them? I understood, but it didn't relieve my anxiety even for a moment. Whatever we might find couldn't be good. That I knew instinctively. Somebody was being paid a chunk of money. I knew Rebekah would start her investigation with or without me, but my guts felt that this would not end well for her, and probably not for us. My imagination couldn't dream up one scenario where this played out for our benefit.

We met in the D/FW terminal on Sunday. She arrived from Boston and I from Lexington as planned. We had a couple of hours before the flight to Buenos Aires, so we found a TGIF and ordered sandwiches. It was good to see her again, even if it had only been a few days. She almost looked herself dressed in jeans and a smartly pressed white collared shirt. She obviously had been catching up on some beauty sleep. I also noted that she had been to a hair salon.

"I'm glad to be going with you, but I'm still unsure what we expect to discover," I said.

"My husband was involved in something that I still don't have a clue about. I have to at least find out what it was," she said.

"What are the options?" I continued to probe.

"I've been thinking about that, too, but I don't have anything that makes sense. If he really was exporting toys, then maybe this was just an automatic payment that was set up for a supplier, and it has just continued," she outlined.

"Why would he hide something like that from you?" I continued to push.

She asked, "What do you think the options are?" She was turning the table on me.

"I didn't know your husband, so it's hard for me to guess, but usually if a man is hiding something from his wife, it has to do with something illegal. Or it involves another woman, but I'm just speculating," I offered.

She responded, "I've thought about both of those. I didn't really trust his brother. I just had a suspicion that he had taken dangerous risks most of his life. That pattern cost him his marriage, and I think it probably cost both his and Gary's lives." I noticed that she really didn't answer my speculation.

"I've had another thought, too," I said. I waited to see if she wanted me to continue.

"Don't leave me in suspense. What else could it be?" she asked.

"The FBI told you after their investigation that they believed that Gary and his brother had been killed, but the bodies were never found. Is that right?" I said.

"Yes, that's right. After a year and a half with no word, I had to believe them," she confessed.

"Why did they think the two were dead? That doesn't seem to be the normal routine to just assume that a missing person is a dead person. They must have found something that led them to such a conclusion, even if they couldn't prove it," I offered.

She nodded in agreement, saying in a hushed tone as she glanced around to be sure no one was listening, "They did. They were holding a man in conjunction with another crime. He told them that Gary and his brother Garrett had been betrayed and executed in Mexico, but that's all the FBI would tell me. They said that to reveal any more would jeopardize their ongoing investigation concerning the other case, but they said they believed the witness's report."

Lost Under the Lion's Shadow

"That may be, but hear me out. What if your husband got in over his head with something, and knew that to continue, he was risking his life and maybe even yours? What if he needed to disappear, or 'die,' to protect himself and maybe you?" I said all of that, but without much conviction.

"You're thinking Gary may not be dead? If that's the case, then the checks to Argentina might be going to Gary himself. Is that what you're speculating?" she asked.

"It doesn't fit any logical pattern. You said that you two always talked about going fishing down in Argentina, but that you never went. Then you find a second passport that indicated that he had been eleven times in three years, but you never knew it. That fishing guide even remembered guiding a Gary from Boston. I'm assuming that you knew that he was gone somewhere," I said.

Rebekah thought for a moment then said, "Before getting mixed up with his brother Garrett, he never left town except with me. He was a CPA with a large Boston firm. Most, if not all, of his clients were in the Boston area, but when he left the firm and joined up with his brother, they started traveling all over the world. They were probably gone once or twice a month usually for a week at a time. I didn't like it, but I trusted my husband," she said trying to whisper, as a couple seated themselves next to our table. Whispering didn't come natural to those who live in Boston.

"I don't think he's alive living down in Argentina," I said with some certainly, "or if he is, why didn't he take his secret, second passport to get into the country?" I let that observation just hang in the air. "For what it's worth, if I was Gary, I wouldn't have left you for any reason whatsoever," I thought to myself, but said it out loud. She blushed, but didn't verbally respond.

"Were the two of you happy?" I asked afraid that I was getting too personal. Rebekah and I had talked every day beside the clear rivers of Patagonia, but we both avoided our pasts and our marriages. Instead of answering, she tapped on my watch. It was time for us to make our way to the gate.

Once we were nestled in our comfortable leather Business Class seats, I waited to see how far our conversation would go. It was time for us to be completely honest with each other, or there wasn't much chance for our relationship to have a future. I was beginning to realize that Rebekah had some shadows in her history, as did I. As we relaxed in silence, it registered with me that not that long ago my whole identity had been wrapped up in being a pastor, and now I was with a woman who seemed to understand my heart, but whom still didn't even know that I had ever been a pastor. It seemed bizarre to think that such was possible.

As we began to roll down the runway, Rebekah and I were holding hands, but my mind was elsewhere. I remembered the philosophical argument from my freshman year over the difference between essence and accident, or in more modern language, essentials and nonessentials. I laughed to myself as I thought about the silly discussions we had concerning whether a chair was still a chair if it had only three legs. However, not long ago without fully realizing it, my own identity was bound around being a pastor and leading a congregation. It had defined who I was, but now without those "legs," I was realizing that I was still Richard. The realization seemed to be a healthy step wherever else it might lead.

As the plane began to level off, Rebekah interrupted my thoughts saying, "Yes, and then no."

"Yes, then no what?" I responded.

"You asked if Gary and I were happily married. Yes, we were happy until those last few years. I didn't like his brother, and I didn't like the way Gary acted when Garrett was around. It was like he became this whole different person. I felt like I was sleeping with a stranger after he had been with his older brother. I tried to warn him, but he wouldn't listen. It's not that we had screaming fights; we just started ignoring certain topics. We quit going to church. We didn't have time for our friends. Gary was always gone or getting ready to leave. At the time I don't think I realized how miserable I had become," she mused.

"So you and Gary went to church?" I asked. It caught me off guard, but I'm not sure why.

"Most of the time, at least for a season. Gary had been raised in one of the high steeple churches in downtown Boston. My family went to a little Baptist church in Indiana before we moved to Pennsylvania. We met each other at Boston College and married after graduation. We went to a little church not too far away from where we lived in Cambridge. There aren't that many active churches in Cambridge, but we liked the pastor and the music. When Gary started getting so busy with his brother, he just seemed to lose interest, and I didn't want to go by myself," she answered.

I nodded with understanding.

"I did start attending another church a few years ago, but I haven't been very involved. Did you and your wife go to church?" she asked in pure innocence.

"Yes, we went to church," I responded without details, resisting the urge to laugh out loud. "Did you and Gary ever have kids?" I asked to change the subject.

"No, something was wrong with one of us, something physically," she said louder than I had wished. "His 'boys' were too sparse, or so the doctor said, but I had some issues, too. Anyway, by the time we realized it wasn't happening, we both seemed to be too busy to do anything about it. We once even discussed adopting, but after agreeing that we were interested, we never discussed it again."

I didn't know how to respond, but I thought about my daughters. I hadn't told them that I was returning to Argentina.

"You had kids didn't you?" she asked seeming to already know the answer.

"Yes," I responded, "Rachel and I had two girls a year apart. They're both married with their own lives now. They make their daddy proud."

"Grandkids?" she continued with a warm smile.

"Not yet, but it wouldn't surprise me to hear something soon. They both want kids and are in a good place in their lives."

"What do you do? I can't believe that I've never asked you that before," she quipped.

"You know me fairly well by now. What do you think I do?" I responded. A little guessing game might be fun. She seemed to relish the thought of trying to sort out who I was, or had been.

"You're not a doctor, lawyer, or cop, but you're not a mechanic or builder either. You might be an engineer, or a business owner. You might even be a banker or stockbroker, but I can't see you locked in an office day after day. However, I'm not sure that I can see you dealing with the public every day either. You're a good listener, but...I'm not sure. Am I getting warm?" she asked.

"Before Rachel died, I pastored a church," I said in a matter-of-fact voice.

"Really? You're a preacher? I never would have guessed that," she said with a chuckle, "but you're not now?"

"I decided that the church needed a pastor with more energy than I had. My wife's cancer drained the life out of me. With our savings, I was able to retire early. It was best for all," I added.

She seemed content with my response, but I did notice that we were no longer holding hands. She probably had misgivings about being "with" a preacher, much less holding hands. As I was sharing all of this with her, I also realized how much I missed the ministry. It really was what I had been called to do, but it felt good to be distant from it for a season. After a surprisingly tasty airline meal and a short nap, we were circling to align into the approach at Buenos Aires. From there Rebekah had arranged a private charter for us. I wondered with some trepidation what that meant in Argentina. I didn't even know where it was planning to take us, but I trusted her.

CHAPTER 6

Bajo Los Caracoles

The 1100-mile flight to Bajo Los Caracoles was rough in the small charter. The view from above confirmed how wide-open and empty the region of Patagonia really was, and yet at the same time amazingly beautiful. The grasses from above ranged from rusty red, to orange, to almost a deep purple. The wind was bucking the Twin Bonanza, leaving us somewhat shaky by the time we finally touched down on the grass strip. Don Mario, driving a 1980's Citroen van, transferred us to the only hotel in the small village, the Hotel Bajo Caracoles. We both nearly laughed out loud when we saw the hotel building.

Over the main door, the year 1943 was carved into stone, but the building appeared to be more of the 1843 vintage. A round antique Coca-Cola sign was attached to the corner of the rock building, but was hanging upside down. It truly was little more than a stone house with a front room containing a small bar, kitchen, back porch and four small bedrooms.

The bathroom was an addition off the back porch. We assumed it had hot running water, but that was a major assumption on our part.

The proprietor, a rather large soft-spoken woman, spoke broken English to get us situated into our room. We had to continue resisting the urge to break out into laughter through the process. The window in our room was draped with a homemade mix of color and textures. It could just have easily shrouded a Gypsy trailer. The bed was a wooden bunk bed with the lower mattress being slightly larger than a twin, but not quite a full. The pictures on the wall over the old desk were faded photos of Mt. Aconcagua, the tallest peak in the Americas, and Iguazu Falls, one of Argentina's more spectacular sights.

When the door closed, Rebekah and I just lost it. The laughter was pent up for far too long. We had been transported back into time, and we wondered what else was in store. We hadn't even talked about room arrangements. I assumed that we would have two rooms, but I was also working under the assumption that we would at least be in a Holiday Inn. I had even thought about how refreshing a dip in the swimming pool would be after the long bouncing flight.

It was a humorous surprise for both of us to discover the range of amenities provided at the Hotel Bajo Caracoles. By the way, the other rooms were undergoing remodeling and not available. If we didn't enjoy and trust each other so much, then this would have been an embarrassing situation, but with good humor, I volunteered to take the top bunk. After a brief walk to the only open eating establishment in town, we tasted the dish for the evening. It was *pollo* and beans, *pollo* and rice, or for a few pesos more, *pollo* with rice and beans.

To our surprise the broiled chicken tasted better than we were expecting, but expectations weren't that high. The Coca-Colas were cool, not cold, served in tall bottles. The next morning a rented vehicle was to be delivered for our use. Rebekah had thought about almost everything. Our scheme was simple. We were going to stake out the local post office until somebody came and took a check from Box 18, and then we were going to follow them to wherever. It wasn't a very sophisticated plan, but after racking my brain, I didn't know how to improve on it.

After talking in the dark for a few minutes over a howling wind rattling the roof, we fell asleep with the help of some Advil retrieved from my shaving kit. The top bunk wasn't going to be kind to my back. The next morning in the bathhouse, I discovered that it did have water, almost hot water. Rebekah had discovered it the night before. The warm shower was just what I needed. When I emerged I was feeling almost human again, and walked back through the hallway into the center room. Rebekah was up, dressed, and visiting with the good-natured proprietor.

In a chipper voice, she asked, "Good morning, honey. How was your shower?"

I assumed that she had decided that it would be better for the village folks to think of us as a married couple. I didn't see any reason to argue.

"It felt great," I responded not exaggerating much.

"I was asking Victoria where in town we could mail a postcard. She has informed me that this is the *Oficina de Correos* and that she is the *Amante de Post.* All of Bajo Los Caracoles comes to get their mail right here," she added.

I noticed that behind Victoria above the counter were a few dozen antique mail slots with numbers barely readable. Post Office Box #18 was in the top row and was noticeably empty. From the bank statements, we knew that the check was sent on the eighth of every month, and it was cashed every month on the twelfth thru the fourteenth, never later and never earlier. Today was the eleventh. Rebekah obviously understood the photographic principle of "bracketing" where a photographer shoots above and below the range hoping to catch the perfect photo. She didn't want us to be late, and that's why we came when we did.

We also discovered that the Hotel Bajo Caracoles provided a breakfast on the back porch. It included a platter of various baked buns and rolls with an assortment of local jams and honey. The honey was too strong for our tastes, but the strawberry jam was marvelous. It tasted like fresh strawberries dipped in a chocolate milkshake. From the back porch area we could see the front counter and even the corner of Box 18.

After we finished our breakfast, Victoria attempted to probe our purpose in visiting her modest village. She wanted us to fully enjoy our stay, though it puzzled her that any tourist would come to visit Caracoles without a specific objective. We listened with pretense as she told of the river to the Northwest, and that many came to fish. Within an hour or so, we could discover Cueva de Las Manos. She explained that it was a very well known example of prehistoric rock art and was maybe 10,000 years old.

She also told us of the coast with its penguins and sea lion colony, but admitted that it was a considerable drive. The actual village of Bajo Los Caracoles probably consisted of fifty structures at the most. We decided to explore the area today, because tomorrow we needed to keep a close eye on Box 18. Our rental car amazingly looked exactly like the Citroen van that brought us from the grass strip yesterday. It had several rusty spots in its forest green paint, but the inside appeared to have been recently cleaned, even since we rode in it yesterday.

After touring the village, which took all of five minutes, we drove out to the river canyon. It was considerably larger than the streams we were fishing slightly more than a week ago. This was a powerful river that one would need to be careful in trying to fish while wading. I would not want to attempt to cross it on foot. Last week we were very serious and prepared to fish, but now we were tourists, or least we pretended to be. We took off our shoes and waded in the cold water along the edge. I suspected that if we had our fly rods, we could have had some excitement right on the spot.

There was something amazing about relaxing while watching the running water. We sat on a grassy bank for about a half-hour just letting the warm sun find our shoulders as the river flowed along eventually reaching the Atlantic. The cool, dry air seemed to make Rebekah's skin glow with health. The tension lines around her eyes were nonexistent while we fished last week, but had become more noticeable when we met in Boston. I could tell they were somewhat less visible now, relaxing beside the river. I knew this to be true, because as she would look away upstream, I studied her facial features carefully. I also privately wondered if the tension lines around her eyes were just a product of living in Boston. She broke the silence saying, "Thanks for coming with me."

"I wouldn't have missed this wild adventure for the world," I responded with a big grin. "Thanks for..." she paused, apparently unsure how to express her thoughts. "Thanks for... I think you know."

"I do?" I asked genuinely unsure what she meant.

"Thanks for being such a gentleman," she finally voiced. I didn't respond except with a gentle nod. She continued, "I believe you know how I feel about you, but there are times and seasons for all things. Thanks for understanding such things."

"I think I understand what you mean, but could I kiss you anyway?" I said with a slight grin.

She started laughing. In her joy she hung her head down, letting her hair fall over her face while still chuckling. When she rose back up, she leaned over and kissed me. For several minutes we ignored the truth that there were times and seasons for all things.

As we walked arm in arm back to our green Citroen, which was considerably covered in dust now, I said, "I was afraid that after you found out that I had been a preacher practically all my life, that I might somehow be tainted, or off limits."

"Off limits?" she asked.

"Some people think there are three genders: male, female and preachers," I said in jest.

She laughed and kissed me on the cheek saying, "I have never doubted that you are a man. My doubts have more to do with me. In the midst of watching my husband spin away from me and into whatever he got himself into, I had real doubts whether I was...how should I say it?"

I relieved her anxiety by interrupting, "I think you're beyond beautiful, and whatever 'it' is, in my mind you still have 'it.' I think you always will."

She laughed the laugh she had laughed all of last week, and then winked at me and said, "Times and seasons..." Rebekah did indeed have a beautiful smile.

When we returned to our not quite five-star accommodations, we both stiffened as we walked past the counter with its makeshift post office. Box 18 clearly had a letter. It looked to be the size and shape of an envelope that would have been mailed from the bank. It was the right time; it had to be the check. Our stakeout was on. If we missed this opportunity, then it would be another month unless we could get Victoria to spill the beans, which we both believed would be doubtful.

The next morning, after our breakfast feast where we focused again on the amazing strawberry jam, we set up our watch plans. Our arrangement was to alternate keeping watch on Box 18 so that it wouldn't be quite so obvious. We would tell Victoria that we needed to spend some time writing and checking our e-mail. We changed that last detail because we hadn't found a strong enough Internet signal as of yet, though Victoria assured us that at certain times of the day, on some days of the month, when the moon is just right, she gets a good signal. I had my doubts.

About midmorning, a middle-aged woman came into the Hotel Bajo Caracoles and local post office. She was the third person to come in to gather their mail and hear the latest gossip from Victoria. I covertly watched her, but quickly concluded that she wasn't there for Box 18. She and Victoria visited about their grandchildren. One of the kids had been sick with some rare disease, and the doctor couldn't decide what it was; but my Spanish was shaky, so I wasn't sure whose child it was, or even whether the baby had recovered.

The two women chatted on in quiet voices for several more minutes. They were obviously gossiping about somebody in town, and didn't want me to overhear the latest juicy news. They weren't sure whether I understood Spanish anyway. I quit paying much attention as they continued getting caught up on all the important local news. When she finally walked out, I glanced up at Box 18. It was empty. I had not even noticed Victoria handing her the letter, but it was gone.

Quickly I stepped into our 'lovely' room. Rebekah was reading her novel. I quietly, but urgently said, "We're on." The woman was already out the door, but she wasn't hard to find. Her bright red pullover sweater and red hair were easy to spot since she was the only person on the streets. We assumed that it was her red four-wheel-drive Toyota Tacoma down the street being filled with gas, but instead of going straight towards it, she crossed the street to the local bank and drug store. We hadn't even noticed the bank before. It didn't seem to have the atmosphere that our hotel did.

She was inside about five minutes, and then she walked past the gas station to the corner store. Ten minutes later with a sack of grocery items, she moved towards her pickup. It appeared to have been ridden over a fair number of miles on the washboard roads of Patagonia.

As she left town heading west, we were behind her in our Citroen. I was somehow relieved and excited. The woman appeared to be completely harmless. How much trouble could we get into? Her plume of dust was easy to follow even from a mile back. The terrain of the Pampas was amazingly flat. About ten miles outside of Bajo Los Caracoles, she turned back to the North on a small lane. It appeared to be a private road leading to a homestead. We decided to stop on the main road and observe. About a mile or so down the lane the dust plume ceased. We couldn't quite see her park because she had disappeared over a ridge, but we knew about where she had stopped.

"Now what do we do?" I asked.

"I'm not sure," Rebekah responded.

We sat on the side of the road for a few more minutes as our own dust plume completely settled. There wasn't any other traffic.

"Let's go meet her," Rebekah finally blurted out, "I have a plan."

"Would you mind sharing it with me?"

"Just continue to pretend to be my husband," she said with a smile.

"I'm good at that," I claimed.

"However, I think we need to give her some time. Now that we know where she is, let's drive on west just to see what we can see," she said.

I shifted the old Citroen into gear, and we continued down the road. In a couple of miles it was clear that the road was bending back to parallel the river. At an overlook point, we could see the river down in the shallow, but wide canyon. Back downstream we could see a house and maybe a barn on the canyon's edge. That was about where our "$15,000 a month" woman stopped.

We waited a couple of hours. It was lunchtime, but there weren't many choices even back in town. I ate an apple from our stash. After Rebekah thought that it had been enough time, we started back towards town. At the Box 18 road, we turned. Driving down the lane Rebekah reached over and squeezed my leg saying, "Thanks for trusting me."

We couldn't see any structure whatsoever until we reached the edge of the river canyon. Just down off the edge were a house and a small barn. The two-story house was nicer and newer than we expected. After our hotel, our expectations weren't very high, but this was tastefully elaborate. The cedar-planked house was split level sloping off the side of the canyon. A large deck was suspended from the second floor. The view from that deck down the river would be tremendous.

"This looks like a $15,000 a month home," I offered being mildly sarcastic.

Rebekah glanced at me with a pretend scolding. We walked up to the front door like we knew what we were doing. Rebekah did, no doubt, but I didn't. The large front porch had a series of attractive pots and planters. Several bright red blooms were peering from the healthy greenery. We waited several minutes after knocking on the door. The door didn't open, but the Box 18 woman leaned over the second floor deck and surprised us. She was still wearing her red pullover. She spoke in elegant *Castillano*, the Argentine version of Spanish, and asked what we needed.

Rebekah led the offense. After stepping back so that we could look up and see her without straining, Rebekah said in English, "We're staying with Victoria at Hotel Bajo Caracoles. We would really like to stay in the area another week or so, but we aren't sure that Victoria has room for us for another week."

The woman was amused and responded also in very good English, "Sure, I saw him this morning," nodding and pointing towards me. "So Victoria's one room with bunk beds isn't comfortable enough?" She had a warm smile on her face and we both nodded with understanding. "What can I do for you?"

"Victoria mentioned that you might offer a room for some newlyweds for a week or so," she lied. It was the first and second lie that I had heard escape from her lips, but she appeared to be a natural.

"Victoria said that? Yes, I did a few years ago, but I really can't any more. Sorry," she said with some firmness.

"You have such a lovely place. Do you have any other recommendations?" Rebekah said. She didn't want to take "no" for an answer.

Box 18 woman turned and left the second floor landing. I assumed that we had been turned down, but Rebekah held her ground, and sure enough the front door opened.

"I'm Regina Mendoza. I'm the caretaker for the *casa*. I'm not supposed to take in guests, but if you're only staying a short time, we might be able to work something out."

After she and Rebekah agreed upon the details, we told Doña Regina that we would be back in a few hours after retrieving our luggage from Victoria's establishment. My back was celebrating that it wouldn't be spending another night on Victoria's top bunk.

CHAPTER 7

Head Lights

After grabbing our gear and explaining our situation to a disappointed but understanding Victoria, we were back on our way towards Regina's. We grabbed some snacks and fruit at the corner grocery, understanding that our accommodations with Regina would include breakfast and dinner, but not lunch, but even that was unclear. It seemed that Argentineans eat on a different schedule than Americans.

When we arrived back to the riverside home, we were again impressed by the structure. In didn't appear to be very old, but the small outbuilding seemed to have been there forever. We surmised that the new home had replaced a much older house that would have been more in keeping with the old barn. Regina greeted us with great hospitality. She obviously had been working with considerable speed to spruce up the place for guests. A bouquet of beautiful, fresh yellow daylilies was the centerpiece on the grand dining table. An amazing hand-carved grandfather clock stood beside the staircase.

Our host led us upstairs. Just as I reached the top of the stairs with our bags, I realized the implication of the lie that Rebekah fabricated. Regina considered us to be middle-aged, second-marriage newlyweds, and thus she was taking us to the master suite. A glance and nod towards Rebekah communicated the irony of this situation. Our host opened the floor length drapes, revealing a wall of glass opening onto the decking. Even from inside it was more than obvious that the view was breathtaking. The canyon was below us with its winding river, but in the far distance one could easily see the snow-capped Andes.

After dropping the luggage beside the bed, I joined the women on the deck. The view was even more than amazing. Regina stepped away, informing us that we had time to clean up before dinner would be served. As she closed the door behind her, she nodded with warmth and humor. It was evident that she enjoyed having guests, especially newlyweds.

Rebekah and I stepped back onto the deck. She looked at me and said, "Not bad, is it, especially for a honeymoon suite?"

Catching her sarcasm, I responded, "I have to hand it to you, you can lie your way into anything, but I really liked Victoria's strawberry jam, and the sway mattress of the top bunk..."

"I knew that you were going to miss that mattress, but the other disappointment I may have an answer for," she said as she walked back inside over to her bags. Just inside the top zipper, she reached in and produced two jars of the amazing local strawberry concoction. "Perhaps you should consider them wedding gifts; after all, we are newlyweds," she added with a whimsical expression.

I hugged her as we both laughed and giggled. My arm remained around her waist as we walked back out on the deck. The sun was starting to put on a show to the West. We both stood there in awe. There was a difference, however. Our week of fishing together had been pure and honest. We didn't talk about our pasts, but our hearts were open and transparent. Now we were living lives of deception and lies. We were on a mission to discover the circumstances surrounding a death, and probably a murder. As beautiful as this view happened to be, in the back of both of our minds there was a dark cloud looming. I longed for the previous perspective.

Regina apologized over and over that she hadn't had time to prepare properly, and that it had been some time since she had been a proper host, yet the meal of blackened salmon and fresh fruit was marvelous. She served us a local white wine, but neither Rebekah nor I really appreciated the beverage, which seemed to disappoint her.

During the entire evening, Rebekah and I both thought about what our next steps ought to be. This sweet and gracious woman was collecting $15,000 monthly from Gary's hidden checking account. Why did he owe her? What was the arrangement? What was really happening behind the scenes? Leisurely, we began to ask Regina some seemingly innocent questions. We learned that she was a native Argentinean, a *porteño*, meaning she was from Buenos Aires. Half of the country's forty million people live in or around the capital.

Her dad had been a captain of a fishing boat, but her mom died in a car wreck in Regina's teen years. She started taking care of houses shortly thereafter. She had been at this house for over six years. The owner used it only as a winter home a few times a year she claimed, but she was paid to take care of the house year round. She seemed comfortable in telling her story as if she had nothing to hide. She would have panicked to know who Rebekah was, and what we knew about the monthly payments, but nothing she said seemed to fit. The puzzle we were trying to piece together didn't have many pieces that were locking collectively.

If the owner seldom used it, but did use it occasionally, and recently, then why was Gary, who supposedly has been dead for four years, still paying for it? It seemed that he was paying off some kind of major debt postmortem. My mind was racing as we listened to Regina share her pride of Argentina. We were able to maintain the charade with our host all evening, giving her no cause for alarm. After we finished the extended meal, Regina suggested that I should move our van around to the back. There wasn't room in the small barn, but squarely behind the barn towards the river would be preferable. I followed her suggestion, not realizing the full motive until the chore was accomplished. She didn't want our lovely green rental to be visible from the front drive. Maybe it conflicted with her sense of beauty and order.

When it was time for bed, we said our good nights and moved up the stairs. Standing out on the deck, we barely could even see where the canyon started because it already was so dark. The stars were absolutely brilliant. The sky of the southern hemisphere was so different compared to the sky I had grown up observing. None of my familiar constellation friends in the heavens were visible. It was a new world down here on the bottom side of the earth.

We held each other for a few minutes. The night air coming down the canyon was much colder than we anticipated. Each night felt colder than the night before. Whispering into Rebekah's ear, I said trying to be humorous, "I'm already missing Victoria's top bunk." She giggled and held me tighter.

"How do you want to sleep? Regina already thinks we're married," she commented. It was too dark outside to know what her face was saying.

"I'll take the sofa," I answered.

"You're such the gentleman, but if you..." she said.

"No ifs or buts," I said. "You're amazing, but it's time for bed. Good night," I said, and I gently kissed her. The sofa wasn't quite long enough, but I didn't complain.

The night was as long as the sofa was short. Not wanting to disturb Rebekah, who appeared to be sleeping soundly in the big four-poster bed, I slipped on my jacket in the dark and stepped out onto the deck. The hooded jacket was just barely enough to fight off the chilly breeze.

Almost immediately after noticing the extent of the blackness, the stars became dimmer. The eastern horizon was almost perceptible. Venus seemed to be brighter. The deck chair wasn't as comfortable as most of the house's furniture, but it would do. Apparently it had been secured more for its style than comfort. As I continued to wait on the morning, I thought I heard someone stirring downstairs. It was very subtle, but I concluded that Regina must be up starting the coffee. I walked around on the deck, away from the bedroom sliding door so that I might have a wider view of the East and perhaps see if lights were on downstairs.

No sooner had I changed positions then I noticed the flash of car lights. Someone was up early on the main road heading into Bajo Los Caracoles. The vehicle itself could not be seen, but the faint beam of its lights into the dark sky was clear, but then it slowed. There was no mistake. The vehicle unquestionably turned down the lane towards our house. I decided to just hold my position, except I eased down into another of the stylish but uncomfortable deck chairs. That put me deeper into the shadows. When the car lights reached the canyon's edge, the sky was starting to get even lighter. The vehicle pulled down to the front of the house.

The front door opened and I saw Regina walking towards the dark sedan. Obviously she had been waiting for its arrival. She was carrying something, but it wasn't light enough to identify. A man dressed in dark clothing stepped out of the still running sedan, but just stood beside the car and waited for her. Words were clearly spoken, although I couldn't hear them, and she handed him whatever she had taken from the house: a book, maybe a magazine or maybe a large envelope. Suddenly the man grabbed her arm and pulled her in close. It wasn't the touch of friendship or romance. He whispered something in her ear before she pulled away, and then as quickly as he arrived, he was gone. The whole event didn't take but just a few minutes, and I didn't know what to make of it, but I had a suspicion that something wasn't right. The hair on the back of my neck was standing on end.

Downstairs, it was now evident that Regina was in the kitchen starting breakfast. I thought that I could smell the aroma of coffee brewing. I wondered what else this day would hold. When I stepped back into the room, I was trying my best to stay quiet, but Rebekah said from the dark, "How was the sofa?"

"Not too bad," I lied.

"You're lying. I can tell. You're not very good at it," she said.

"I disagree, I think I'm fairly good at it. After all, I was a preacher for over twenty years," I said as I sat down on the edge of the large bed. The morning was getting much lighter, and I was missing the sunrise.

"Are you saying that preachers lie?" she asked.

I realized that I needed to explain. "As a pastor you must learn to couch your words. There are times to be gut-level honest, but you need to have earned that right in a relationship. A pastor who speaks what he thinks about a situation, without having earned that right, stays continually in hot water," I explained.

"Have you been less than honest with me, waiting to earn the right?" she asked with a slight giggle.

I responded, "Probably we both have."

Before this embarrassing conversation was able to go much further, the phone beside the bed rang. We both looked at each other somewhat confused in the pale morning light. Rebekah picked it up and said, "Hello?" She nodded and smiled as she reported, "Our host says that breakfast is ready when we are." As she tiptoed to the bathroom, I noticed a ceramic lion standing in the corner. I'm not sure why, but it's presence gave me a strange sense of comfort.

CHAPTER 8

Disclosure

Breakfast was outstanding. Regina was truly a professional host with much experience, but she wasn't as chipper and talkative as she had been last night. She explained to us that most Argentineans eat breakfast later in the morning, with the afternoon lunch being the major meal, but she assumed that as Americans we would prefer the normal American schedule. As I finished my third and final slice of French toast, Regina explained that we were not going to be able to stay another night. She was very apologetic, but something had changed. I had to assume that it had to do with the early morning visitor.

Rebekah seemed to be speechless and unsure how to continue, but I knew that we needed to be upfront, and that now was the time. I hadn't had the opportunity to mention the incident of the early visitor to Rebekah.

"Earlier this morning you handed a man something out on the driveway. He had some words to say, and seemed to be upset about something. What is wrong?" I asked.

Regina looked shocked. She clearly didn't think we had seen her visitor, but finally responded, "He represents the owner, and they plan to bring some guests tomorrow. That's why you two will have to leave."

"So the owner and guests are coming tomorrow?" I asked.

She nodded her head to say yes, but didn't offer any other explanation.

"Who is the owner of the house?" I decided to go for the throat.

"He's an American," she answered, but again that's all she offered.

Now was not the time to back down. "Is he a man named Gary Black?" I asked.

She stood there at the oven for a moment with her back towards us. She was the one now confused, and then turned quickly towards us and snapped, "How do you know Señor Black?" There was considerable apprehension in her voice and face.

Rebekah jumped in, "I'm Rebekah Black; Gary was my husband." The grandfather clock started chiming from the next room to break the tense silence.

Regina sat down. Her face was pale, but she said, "Señor Black never said anything about being married. He never brought a wife, or even mentioned a family, and he has been here many times since I started to work at his house. I know him very well. He is a very good man, a true gentleman. I don't believe you. Why are you here?" It was evident that she was a very loyal employee and ready to defend what she thought to be right no matter the consequences.

"That's why we are here. I want to know what happened to my husband. I want to know what Gary was involved with. I loved him very much," Rebekah said glancing my direction hoping that last statement hadn't stung too much.

"Has something happened to Señor Black? Where is he? What happened?" Regina said with genuine worry on her face.

I went on to explain that we didn't know, but decided that at least for now we wouldn't mention the FBI reported speculation.

"How did you find this place? How did you find me?" Regina asked.

I glanced at Rebekah. She nodded and then she answered, "Regina, I found a checking account that belonged to my husband. The bank has been sending $15,000 monthly to Box 18 at the post office at Hotel Bajo Caracoles for at least four years. That is your post office box. We watched you pick up the check and take it to the bank. We followed you out here to the house."

Regina had nothing to say, but I did, "When was the last time you remember seeing Señor Black?"

She hesitated. It was apparent that she was being forced to make a major decision. Could she really trust us? In reading her face, it reflected that she didn't have many others that she could trust. She eventually said, "It's been almost a year. I fear that something has happened to him. Señor Black is a very kind and generous man, but his friends are not." She was trying to be careful in her wording. Her words were subtle, but her face showed real fear. "*Hombres crueles*," she whispered.

"Are you sure that it has been almost ONE year?" Rebekah said with more passion than she intended.

"*Si*, I'm sure. He loved my special Easter *parrilla*; it was my papa's favorite. It's a chorizo stuffed shrimp with smoked prosciutto. Gary could eat a bucket load. I prepare that dish every Easter in honor of my *padre*. Señor Black was here the last time I cooked *parrilla* for Easter. He has not been back since. I have not heard from him since. His associates have come, but not Señor Black," she explained.

"Not since Easter almost one year ago..." Rebekah said to herself again. I couldn't tell whether she was angry, or terribly sad, or just processing. The news was not what she had expected in any shape or form. She was prepared to hear a report of his death, but news of his life left her unbalanced.

"Tell us about the checks," I continued.

Regina was ready to talk. "The check comes every month. I cash it at Carlos'. He keeps part of it, and pays all the house bills. I take part of it for food and upkeep on the house. I was told to keep an additional $500 for me. The remainder, usually about $12,000, is put in an envelope, and one of Señor Black's associates comes by and I give it to him. That's who you saw this morning. It's been that way ever since I started keeping the house," she explained.

"The man this morning seemed to be irritated. He grabbed your arm and said something to you. Why was he angry? Did he threaten you?" I asked.

"As I said before, Señor Black is a good man, but some of his friends are *medios*; they're mean. The man who comes each month would not be happy to know that you were here. If he found out what I've told you, he would be very angry," Regina said. We both noticed that she didn't really answer my question, but I let it go.

"Before last Easter, before he stopped coming, how often would Señor Black come to the house?" I asked still trying to get a picture of the complex situation.

Without hesitation Regina shared, "Eight or nine times a year for about a week or two at a time."

"When he came, what did he do?" I continued to push, "Did he come alone, did he sit around and read, or did he go places and just use the house as a base?"

"He would come and relax, but he loved to go fishing in the rivers. Sometimes he was gone all day, but he always seemed to be full of joy," she explained. That last statement was a dart towards Rebekah, though Regina hadn't intended it to be so.

"However, something had happened the last few times he came. He seemed moody, almost sad. He didn't always eat my meals, and that was never the case before. He barely even touched the stuffed shrimp at Easter. It was as if he was worried about something, but he never said anything to me," Regina responded.

"Did he leave anything here at the house, such as any personal papers, or business papers?" I wondered not expecting a positive answer. Rebekah looked impressed at my question.

At first Regina paused. To say anything would be to betray the owner of the house, and she was loyal.

He had been good to her. She finally asked, "What has happened to him?"

"The US government thinks that he was killed, maybe executed," Rebekah said. She pulled from her purse a copy of Gary's death certificate and handed it to Regina. She studied it carefully.

Rebekah was hoping that she wouldn't notice the date variance. It was issued a year and a half after he didn't come home to Boston, but that's almost two years before last Easter. However, Regina didn't notice the date, or at least didn't do the math.

"*Muerto*, Senor Black is *muerto*," Regina said to no one in particular. "I suppose that makes you the owner of this house. That makes you my boss," she said.

As odd as it may sound, such a conclusion had not entered into Rebekah's imagination until that moment. I couldn't say the same. I could tell that Rebekah was chewing on the prospect. It was a beautiful place, but was it really hers?

Regina continued, "There is a safe in the closet in the downstairs office. The office is where he spent most of his time when he was here, but I don't know the combination of the safe. He never told me."

All three of us went down the hallway towards the office. It had a big impressive window overlooking the river, and a sliding glass door that was directly underneath the master bedroom upstairs where we had spent the night. The small, but solid safe was where Regina said it would be. It was hidden behind an old coat that was hanging from a wooden peg. Rebekah recognized that coat as one of Gary's. She thought for sure that it had been in a load that she had taken to the Salvation Army, but here it was. It was a modern digital safe, and appeared to have been built into the wall from the initial construction. The three of us stared at it, as if somehow, the longer we stared at the lock it might open all by itself.

Rebekah suddenly said, "I have an idea. This is the office Gary used?" Regina nodded affirmative.

Rebekah immediately walked back into the office and turned over the desk chair to examine the seat bottom. Nothing was taped to the underneath side, but as she studied it, she noticed that on the manufacture's tag, there were three faint numbers in pencil: 12, 28, and 88.

After discovering the numbers and reading them out loud, she froze before finally whispering, "That's our anniversary, December 28, 1988."

I punched in the numbers into the safe. The cylinders began to turn and the door opened. There were only four objects inside: another Beretta 9 mm, another check book from the secret checking account in Boston, another passport, and a black ledger book of some sort. The passport was Gary's. He evidently had at least three such documents, maybe more. A quick glance revealed several more visa stamps from Argentina, and then several more into France and Bulgaria. Gary had been quite the traveler.

A cursory glance at the ledger revealed that it had been used to track some kind of inventory. There were dates, and numbers, and perhaps some kind of pricing column, but it was abbreviated so it didn't automatically open itself as to its meaning. There wasn't a hint of any kind that defined what was being inventoried, but the ledger did track for over three years stopping just before last Easter.

"Regina," I said as we moved back to the kitchen area, "do you really expect that Señor Black's "associates" will come tomorrow?"

"No, I lied. He never said anything about coming tomorrow, or anytime, but you still don't want to be here if he or his friends come," she replied with fear in her voice.

"Why?" Rebekah interjected. "What do you know about them that you haven't told us?"

"I really don't know them at all. The last few times any of them physically stayed here at the house was over a year ago. It was apparent to me that there was a real tension between them and Señor Black. I didn't overhear any specifics, but Señor Black seemed to be very worried about something. The others consumed more alcohol than usual," Regina answered.

Rebekah said, "Regina, if you were us, what would you do?"

She didn't hesitate to answer, "Leave. Leave today, and never come back. Something evil is brewing here. I don't know what it is, and neither do you, but I know it's dangerous, very dangerous. Except for Señor Black, they are not good men, *muy malos.*"

"Do you know where we can find them?" I asked.

She looked at me in disbelief, and said, "Didn't you understand what I meant?" I had, and to be honest I wanted to follow her advice.

I decided I needed to go stretch my legs outside. Rebekah continued talking with our host to see what else she might discover. I circled the house, and didn't really see much of interest. There was no landscaping, just rocks and wild grasses. A small path led to the ancient barn that was hiding our rental. It looked like it had been used for livestock at one time, but obviously wasn't used now for much of any thing.

The swinging door was latched, but not locked. I peered inside the darkness. At first I didn't see much, but as my eyes adjusted, I could see several pieces of old furniture stacked to the ceiling. None of it appeared to be of much value. However, after further investigation, there were several old wicker bottom chairs, and even a few old cowhide bottom straight-back chairs. I remembered sitting in one of those when I was a kid at my grandparents' farm. I loved those chairs. They might be of some worth in an antique store back in Lexington.

As I turned to leave, I noticed two plastic bags just inside the door. One of them was filled with several old fly reels, used lines and a broken fly box. It would be fun to look at those in the light, but maybe later. The big fish of Patagonia had obviously worn out some expensive reels.

The other bag contained a well-used canvas fishing vest. I pulled the vest out and examined it. Such a vest was essentially a great big pocket filled with dozens of small pockets both inside and out. I had one nearly like it back in Lexington, but mine wasn't nearly as well used. The pockets were filled with the usual gear a fly fisherman packs: clippers, floatant, small rusty pliers, several rolls of leader materials, and other assorted tackle. I started to fold it back up, but as I tried, I felt something in one of the inside chest pockets.

It was a small notebook in a sealed baggie. I opened the baggie, and flipped open the journal to a middle page and read, "Upper Rio Negro tributary, 45 bows and browns, various white winged dries, considerable hatch on surface." Then it was dated. It was a fly fishing journal. Gary kept a record of his fishing trips. This would be an interesting read for someone who loved to fish. I replaced it in its baggie, but slipped it into my back pocket. I wasn't sure how Rebekah would receive it, but I was very interested.

After walking around the whole property, and seeing nothing of interest, I started back to the house. All over the area were small pieces of rusted iron: nuts, bolts, wire and then a horseshoe. This land had been used as a farming or ranching operation at one time, long before the new house was built, but that probably had no bearing on the current situation; however, one notices details of the past when one sees things through the possibility of a future. I wondered what else Rebekah might have discovered from visiting with Regina without me.

CHAPTER 9

Visitors

When I reentered the cedar-planked house, Rebekah and Regina were sitting in the front room. Regina had been crying. Rebekah explained to me that she was terrified of what would happen to all three of us if the "associates" found us here. I was feeling guilty, as I sat down across from them. Our presence had changed her life, maybe forever.

For the next hour or so, Regina started asking Rebekah questions. She wanted to know about Señor Black's life back in the States. Did he have kids? What was his job? When did she and Gary marry? Why didn't Rebekah ever come with him?

She seemed satisfied with all of Rebekah's answers, and then she pointed to the two of us and asked, "So the two of you aren't really married, or are you?"

Rebekah looked at me, and then explained about how we met on the fishing trip two weeks ago, and how she asked me to come and help her discover the

78

mystery of what happened to Gary. But she said, no, we weren't married because I hadn't asked her.

That last phrase caught me off guard and I choked, but before I could find the right words to respond, she removed me from the hook saying, "I was kidding, but Richard is a dear friend, and someday there might be a time and season." I started breathing again.

Regina decided that we could stay another night or two, simply because none of us knew where else to go. She was still very concerned, but somehow she felt safer with us than without. She cooked a very special afternoon lunch of *locro* stew. It was a tasty combination of potato, corn and chorizo. A dip of *"dulce de leche"* pudding topped it off. Again she apologized for not being prepared for guests. We couldn't imagine the treat it would have been had she been prepared.

Rebekah had the desire to rummage through Gary's office. She seemed to want to be alone, so I left her thumbing through the few dozen books, mostly novels, after searching through every drawer. Upstairs I found the uncomfortable deck chair with the amazing view, holding a cold glass of lemonade. As I studied the river below, I thought about how it ought to be fished. A person would almost have to have a drift boat of some sort. It was too big a river to really fish properly just by wading.

As I was thinking about how to approach it, I remembered Gary's fishing journal. I retrieved it from my pocket and started reading. A quick review reflected that Gary had fished at least a few hours almost every day that he was in Patagonia. At least it appeared that way. Whatever business brought him here didn't require a great deal of personal time, and hardly got in the way of his fishing.

He kept records of the flies used both successfully and unsuccessfully. He noted memorable events of fish that got away, or other interesting things he saw on the river. He even wrote down thoughts he had of how to improve his fishing techniques. Glancing through it, I realized that I would have liked Gary. He was my kind of man, at least when it came to fishing. He would have been fun to fish with. It amazed me that he could be living such a secret life and never let it slip to the surface. It amazed me that he would even have had a desire to do so.

I flipped through the journal to the last entry. It was dated on a Friday. A check on my phone calendar confirmed that it had been Good Friday, the Friday before last Easter. He didn't catch many fish. Instead there was a small note that read, "G's a bastard." That didn't make any sense to me, but it did raise a question that I hadn't considered. Did Gary have friends he fished with? We had already met a guide farther south who remembered a Gary from Boston, but there were three years of fishing trips recorded in the journal. Fishing partners would have been something that Gary would have wanted to remember. Surely he didn't fish by himself on every trip.

As I glanced back through the small journal, I noticed that in the margins on most of the days there were small letters. That had to be a record of those he fished with, but the simple letters A, J, G and LG didn't expose those details to anybody except Gary himself. "G" was probably his brother, Garrett, but other than that, it was a mystery, one of many. Suddenly it dawned on me that in all of our discussions with Regina, we hadn't mentioned Garrett. Did he ever come to the house? Did he fish? Did he meet the same fate as the FBI has proposed for Gary? Did that last entry in the journal refer to his brother? If so, why?

I went back downstairs and found Rebekah. She was reading one of the books that had been on Gary's desk. It was a spy novel about some Nazi hunter after WW II. When she saw me she said, "Do you know that many Nazis came to Argentina after the war to escape their war crimes? There's even a rumor that Adolf Hitler and Ava Braun really didn't commit suicide in the Berlin bunker; those were their doubles. They were able to escape to Argentina. Do you know where it is rumored that they lived until the end of the 1960's?"

"No," I confessed that I didn't know.

"In a mountain chalet about six miles south of Bariloche," she said.

"You learned all of that in that novel?" I asked with raised eyebrows.

"Yes, in a way. There's a newspaper clipping that was being used as a bookmark, a clipping from the Boston Herald over fifteen years ago," she said. "Don't you find that interesting?"

I didn't answer her question, but no, I didn't. However, I did say, "Do you have those pictures with you?"

"The pictures of Gary?" she asked. I nodded.

"Yes, they're in my purse," she said and reached for it.

"I have a hunch," I said, "let's go find Regina."

She was in the kitchen kneading bread dough. The warm yeast smell was inviting and reminded me of my mom. With her hands covered in flour, I held up a photo of Gary and Rebekah together so she could see.

She nodded and said, "*Si, Si,* Señor Black was a handsome man. They made a beautiful couple."

Then I held up another photo.

Regina had an immediate reaction. "He's one of Señor Black's 'associates,' and in my opinion he is *hombres crueles,* maybe the meanest of the group. Señor Black seemed to be more frustrated with him than any of the others. So you know this man?"

I flashed the photo to Rebekah. It was the photo of Gary and Garrett standing together. Regina didn't even know that Gary and Garrett were brothers, and in her opinion Gary feared him. This was getting even weirder. That knot in my stomach was returning. Regina had warned us. Why had we not listened? I knew why.

As we approached bedtime, Regina asked in a very polite way what we wanted to do as far as sleeping arrangements. Now that she knew that we weren't newlyweds, or even married, she didn't want to assume anything. I thanked her for being such a wonderful host, and asked if the smaller bedroom upstairs might be available. She grinned with relief, and started up the stairs to make it ready. It didn't take her long.

The smaller bedroom also had a sliding glass door leading to the deck, but without the wall of glass. After moving my bags over to the smaller room, I stepped outside onto the deck. Rebekah was waiting for me.

We discussed all that we had learned over the course of the day. It was informative, but what's next was less than clear. Where should we go from here?

I wanted to drive south and see if we could find that other fishing guide that remembered a Gary from Boston, but what could he really have told us? What could he have possibly known that would be helpful? We already knew that Gary fished almost every day while he was here. It didn't seem promising, but if not that, what? Perhaps the morning would offer more clues or directions.

We stood outside in the night air holding each other while watching the stars. In the dark I commented, "You caught me off guard with your offhand comment about why we weren't married."

She laughed and poked me in the arm. "You and I both know there are times and seasons," she said softly. We kissed, I tucked her into bed, and then I headed to the other room.

Early the next morning, I was awake at my usual hour. Again I found the deck chair positioned to watch the transition into the new day. I kept glancing back towards the main highway expecting to see another set of headlights, but none were visible. I thought through all that we knew, but confessed to myself that we were near a dead end. It was frustrating because I could feel that we were very close, but where to now? We didn't have any other real clues.

We believed that Gary was dead. We had no evidence that he wasn't, but to close this chapter, Rebekah really needed some more details, as difficult as they might be to face. How could she move on with her life until more answers were produced? I wanted to help her to discover and understand. I had motive, as I glanced towards her bedroom door. I'm not sure how long I sat there, but the darkness was holding on longer than yesterday. I heard no movement downstairs, nor had I seen any sign of Rebekah. Yet suddenly, like it was orchestrated, the eastern sky appeared lighter. It was comforting to see the transformation.

Out of habit I glanced south towards the main road. There still were no headlights visible, yet as I confirmed that no one was coming to join us, something caught my eye. The front driveway looked different, but it was just barely light enough to see. What was out of place? I studied the area for several minutes before I realized what I was seeing. There was a car parked in the circle drive almost hidden in the shadows. Somebody was already here at the house. My heart started to pump. I tiptoed to Rebekah's bedroom glass door. I knew that she wouldn't have locked it. Inside, I leaned over and gently whispered to her. She roused, trying to understand what I was attempting to say. "Somebody is here at the house. We need to get dressed and get prepared."

My adrenaline was pumping. I stuck the Beretta we had taken from the safe in my belt. My jacket would keep it hidden, but I wasn't sure what good it would do. We hadn't found any ammo for it. I suggested that maybe Rebekah should stay upstairs and let me go investigate who it was and what the situation might be, but she wouldn't hear of it. She had no fear, and she wasn't going to miss whatever was about to unfold. I couldn't say the same.

As we started down the stairs, we noticed that most of the downstairs lights were not burning, as they had been the morning before. Only the kitchen light was glowing. At the base of the stairs, we could see across the great room into the kitchen. Regina was sitting alone at the table with her back to us. Seeing her just sitting indicated that something wasn't right.

As we stepped up behind her, I said, "Good morning, Regina." She didn't turn around, but continued with her head down in her hands. Was she crying?

Stepping closer, I then saw a man standing across the kitchen next to the oven. He said, "Good morning, you two love birds. We decided to let you sleep in this morning. Doña Regina has been telling me a very interesting story about you two. We didn't know that Mr. Black still had a family. It's wonderful to meet you, Mrs. Black."

Rebekah responded, "Who are you? How do you know Gary? Where is my husband?"

"Hold your horses. We'll have plenty of time to answer all your questions, plenty of time," he said with a cruel smile. He appeared to be European, but spoke with very little accent. A scar across his left cheek made his smile appear more sinister. His shoes appeared to be high-priced Italian, but they were dusty nevertheless.

"Doña Regina, these good people are hungry. You need to pull yourself together and cook us some breakfast."

She didn't hesitate, but as she stood, we noticed her face. Her cheek was bright red and her eye was starting to swell. Our visitor had clearly slapped her around. I could feel a mix of anger and fear start to well up inside. Was it because of us? What's next for all of us? What had she told him?

CHAPTER 10

Baca Grande Estancia

He motioned for us to take seats at the table Regina had vacated. I started praying to myself. It was the first time that I had felt the need or desire to pray in several months. Rebekah broke the silence. "Who are you and what are your plans?" she tossed out to the visitor.

He didn't hesitate to answer, "Doña Regina had a good thing going on until you two showed up, but now you have gone and crapped in her cake. Just look at her beautiful face. It's such a shame."

Regina didn't look away from the stove as she scrambled some eggs with chorizo.

"In reality, your showing up has fouled things up for everybody, and that's not good for any of us. My friends aren't going to be happy with you," he said menacingly.

"Where's Gary? Where's my husband?" Rebekah said with more anger than fear.

"He's dead, but you already knew that," the visitor snapped.

Rebekah persisted, "What was he involved with?"

The visitor erupted with a cruel chuckle before saying, "Your husband was involved with us of course." He continued to find the question and his answer amusing.

Regina served breakfast, but neither Rebekah nor I could manage a bite. Our minds were spinning trying to think about what we should do. We had the sensation that the visitor didn't plan to allow us to walk away, but he hadn't actually said so. We needed to press the issue to see where we stood.

I stood up and said, "Rebekah and I have plans to fish today. Our guide will be expecting us. We better get started." Regina glanced our direction with her eyes raised.

The visitor started laughing again, and said, "The fish aren't biting today I fear."

"Well, we still need to go meet our guide," and I helped Rebekah to her feet from the table. As we turned towards the great room, we noticed two other men emerging from the office and coming towards us. One was holding a small revolver pointed in our vicinity.

The visitor suggested that we ought to come back, sit down and maybe even finish breakfast. He indicated that it was going to be a long day, and that Regina's chorizo and eggs might be the last chance for nourishment for some time. We understood his veiled threat, but still we didn't have appetites.

He continued, "We have an hour or so before our friends arrive, so you need to answer a few questions. Why did you really come?"

Neither of us spoke. Truthfully, we weren't sure ourselves why we had come.

"It wasn't to find Mr. Black. You knew he was already dead. According to Doña Regina, you even brought a death certificate. So why would you come?" he rambled mostly to himself.

We still didn't answer.

"So I thought to myself. Maybe you came to claim this beautiful home, but again it appears that you didn't even know about this house, so that can't be true. I think that I know. I think that you came for the money. It would solve all of us some serious headaches if you told us right now where it is," he continued to ramble.

We both immediately thought about the two million dollars in the newly discovered checking account back in Boston. Gary must have stolen that money from his associates, but again we said nothing.

He continued, "Actually we could care less about the money. It's a chunk of change, but in the grand scheme of things, it's not all that important. Our business alone clears that much in just a few weeks, but it is the principle of the thing. We can't let one of our own go rogue with business funds. You understand that, don't you?"

"I know where the money is," Rebekah blurted out.

"Really? So where it is?" the visitor asked.

"It's in a checking account in Boston. If I had access to the Internet, I could have the bank wire two million dollars to any account you prefer. Just let the three of us be on our way. We'll go back home and forget about all of this. Regina can even live with me," she said.

"Two million dollars? Don't be jerking me around! You'll wire me two million, but keep the other thirty million? That's a deal that I can refuse," he said while laughing his cruel laugh.

"Two million, that's all I know about," Rebekah said with uncertainty in her voice.

"That may be, but we have to be sure. We have developed a unique way to force a person to confess. It takes some time, but we have time, and our method has been generally effective. I think that may be your transportation now," he said while listening to what sounded like another car pulling up out front. He left to meet the newcomers, but the two men behind us remained. We still couldn't eat.

In a few minutes he returned and asked why we weren't packed yet. His sense of humor needed work, but he suggested that we go upstairs and pack our bags quickly. He followed us up and watched us as we stuffed our minimal belongings in our bags. He didn't seem to care about the cell phones or laptop. He knew that where we were going there would be no service. He ushered us back down the stairs. Regina was nowhere to be seen. In the driveway was the late model black sedan that I had seen twice now. Behind it was a Mercedes delivery van without markings. The rig seemed to be very well used.

With the three "visitors" following us out of the house, there were two others with the delivery truck. The one walking behind us carried the only gun visible, but we both assumed that everybody was armed but us. I didn't count the unloaded Beretta still in my belt.

The back of the truck was opened and we were invited to enter. We didn't have much choice. The door closed and locked behind us. It was almost pitch black inside the locked truck until our eyes adjusted. Nothing was said to us, and in a few minutes the truck started to roll. We could feel the truck drive down the private lane before pulling onto the main road. We sensed that we turned the opposite direction from Caracoles.

The roads had been rough in the Citroen van, but in the back of the delivery truck the washboard roads rattled our teeth. We had no idea what to expect. My imagination ran from the language of the FBI report of "execution," to the article I read in the *Wall Street Journal* about the hostage business in South America. Rebekah and I tried to talk, but it was impossible to hear each other. The truck was flying down the long stretches of the open prairie road. On turns, we had to hold each other to keep from being thrown to the sides.

We both prepared ourselves for whatever was to come, but we weren't ready for the hours of uncertainty. We found it easier to lie down on the used strip carpet on the truck floor than to try to sit up against the wall. As we lay together, I think both of us shed a few tears and said a few prayers. With Rebekah attempting to sleep, I studied the wall of the truck in the dim light. A square of used cardboard was duck-taped to the sidewall. Printed on the cardboard was a lion, the mascot of some Argentine brand. The lion appeared to be running along side us as the truck bounced. At first it was entertaining, but as time passed, it was somehow more than that.

Finally the truck came to a stop. We stood and stretched our legs, expecting the door to open for whatever faced us, but the truck started moving again. That was nearly more than either of us could take. Then it stopped again. It was obvious that we were going through some kind of gate that had to be opened. I tried to peer through the vent in the ceiling, but all I could see was the hint of blue sky. Suddenly the door opened, and we were invited to relieve ourselves if we so needed. Rebekah took one side of the truck and the three of us used the other. There was absolutely nothing to be seen in any direction but the mountains to the west. We were now significantly closer to the peaks. The black sedan that I assumed had been following us was nowhere to be seen.

The truck started again, but this time the road was significantly rougher. We bounced around in the back to the point of bruising, but still we continued without rest. At last the truck slowed down, took several tight turns and then came to a stop. The engine was turned off. We could hear the two men speak, but we could understand not a word. We didn't even recognize the language. The door opened. By then we had decided that they were not going to shoot us. It made no sense to travel this far just to hide the bodies, but what were they planning? When we stepped out of the truck, we were somewhat surprised to step onto thick green grass. All around were tall trees with a small, clear stream running through their midst. Tall cliffs were on either side jutting almost straight up.

The two men walked us through the trees, and we all stepped across the small stream on rocks well-positioned. About seventy-five yards into the thick trees was a small one-room log cabin. It looked to be straight from the old American West. They marched us to the cabin and opened the door. We peered in. It was horribly nasty. The dust was thick, and spider webs filled the air. They pointed to the door where a letter was nailed. It was addressed to us. They motioned that we should enter the cabin and read it.

As we moved through the cobwebs, the door closed behind us. In a few moments we heard the truck roar back to life, back away, and head out the way it had come. I rushed to the door half expecting it to be locked, but it flew open. In the distance I could see the dust plume of the Mercedes truck already out of sight.

"They just left us here," I said to the open door, but Rebekah heard me. With the letter, we both walked back to the small stream and looked around in a state of absolute bewilderment.

The cliffs above us were indeed almost straight up, but the canyon continued back into the mountains for at least another quarter mile. Without saying anything, we followed the stream up to a small meadow. A waterfall was descending from an upper level, falling straight down at least sixty feet. The pool at its base was clear and deep. If we had been in any other circumstance, it would have been one of the most scenic and beautiful places either of us had ever experienced. There was a fallen log at the base of the meadow, so we sat down and caught our breaths, taking in the moment. Every day we had been in Argentina, the sky had been deep blue and almost cloudless. Now it appeared that a dark bank of clouds was moving in. It seemed somewhat appropriate.

Eventually we opened the letter. It had been written on an older typewriter and read:

Welcome to the Baca Grande Estancia,

The Baca Grande is one of the largest ranches in all of Argentina. You are in a box canyon with but one way out. It's about eighty miles to the ranch gate, and another eighty to the main highway.

Here is the situation. Mr. Black, your husband, swindled from us over thirty million dollars. He had to pay the price. We don't know if you know where he hid the money, and we don't know how much you know of our business. Either way, it's best for us if you disappear until we figure these things out.

The rules of the house:

First, it's at least 160 miles to the main road. Even that road sees little traffic. If you care to walk out, you're welcome to try, but we left no water carrier for your travel, so we advise you to think carefully before making such an attempt.

Second, winter often sets in early in these canyons. There may be heavy snow in less than a month. Our advice is to spend the time wisely preparing for the cold. Most of our guests didn't survive the winter snows because they didn't prepare, but we've never had the privilege of entertaining a couple before.

Third, there is enough food for a month if you eat wisely. Another food shipment will arrive every thirty days weather permitting, except the amount of food will be cut back every month you decide not to tell us where the money is hidden.

Fourth, if you decide to tell us the truth, raise the flag that is at the front gate and we will come to visit. If you raise it without the correct information, you will die.

Fifth, and lastly, as long as you desire and are comfortable, you may be our guests.

Your friends of the Baca Grande

Neither of us knew what to say. I read the letter again in silence. The impact of the situation left us struggling to think. The sweet sound of the running water was refreshing, but it was beginning to grow dark. Daylight in the canyon was going to come late and set early. A slight breeze was coming down the canyon into our faces. Perhaps the dark clouds were a harbinger to an early winter. We needed to prepare for the evening, but after today we had little energy. Fear has a way of draining the life from your spirit; our spirits were more than drained. Eventually we went back to the cabin and started sweeping out the cobwebs.

It was almost tolerable when we tumbled into each other's arms and fell onto the bare mattress. I knew that I loved Rebekah, but this was not how I expected our future to unfold. I tried to pray, but I remembered that I had already prayed twice today. Once was at the breakfast table, and the next was in the back of the delivery truck. Both times I asked God to protect both of us, but had he heard my prayers? Of course he did, didn't he? Doubts haunted me.

I had preached hundreds of sermons about faith, but I just lay there wondering if God even knew where we were. When I came down here to fish, I remembered that my goal was to disappear, but this was considerably more than I had bargained for.

CHAPTER 11

Essentials

We were both exhausted. We tried to sleep holding each other, but it wasn't romantic, it was survival. We didn't have light, or fire, or even a blanket for warmth. We piled our clothes over us, but it was cold. The place was so filthy, that by the time we swept it out, it was dark, cold and much dustier. We both coughed ourselves into a sleepless slumber. Sometime in the early morn, I had to breathe some fresh air. The early morning darkness wasn't as dark as I expected because the moon was shining down into the canyon. There was a split log bench on the small porch, and I found it to be more comfortable than the deck chairs at Regina's.

All night I felt like I was in an emotional fog. I couldn't think. Bouncing around in the back of that delivery truck for that many hours simply took the life juices out of both of us, but this morning, surprisingly, I felt awake and ready. My mind was sorting through the various things that had to be done. Yes, we needed to discuss what our plan of action should be, but while we pondered such things, we needed to be sure that we were prepared for whatever came. Those heavy clouds that moved in at dusk last night had obviously moved on during the night, but at this time of the year in this country, you could experience a severe winter storm at any time. The letter suggested that we might have a month, but that was no guarantee.

When it was barely light enough, I started splitting firewood. My mind was racing with all the various things that needed to be taken care of, but firewood was as good as any place to start. There was a massive pile of big logs up against the side of the canyon with an axe buried into a chopping post. From the look of the quantity of chips on the ground, it was clear that several others had been in the same predicament as we were. As I chopped, I was assuming that somewhere we would find matches.

The letter said that there was a food supply for a month, but in our quick cleaning, we hadn't discovered a food cache. When it was full light, we would need to take an inventory of our canyon. What did we have? I had a fair stack of fresh split wood piled up on the front porch before I heard any stirring from inside. Perhaps my stomping around on the porch contributed to her coming out of her deep sleep.

When I saw her face, I realized that I was the one in panic mode. In my mind we had a hundred things to do; our lives were in serious jeopardy. We didn't have time to sleep in, but as I looked at Rebekah's eyes, I realized that I was the one who needed to slow down. We needed to sort this all out together, but I continued chopping and stacking as if I was in a marathon. She sat down on the bench wrapping my jacket around her legs, and just watched my feverish, and if I might add, impressive, wood splitting.

Eventually she said, "What are we going to do?"

I paused with the axe suspended over my head before I let it drop to the ground. I noticed that I had already worn at least one blister in my palm. I joined her on the porch. The morning light had just chased away the shadows.

"Have you stumbled across a food pantry over there by the log pile?" she asked with perhaps a touch of disdain. I admitted that I had not.

"Matches?" she added. I shook my head again.

"Perhaps we best start looking for food and matches," she suggested. The fear and lack of sleep were starting to take their toll on both of us. I stood her up from the bench and hugged her.

Whispering into her ear I said, "I don't know what they expect from us, and I don't know how this will all play out in the end, but let's stick together; you and me, together. Are you with me?"

She nodded and hugged me tighter.

"Do you think they want us to try to walk out?" she asked.

I answered, "I don't know what they want. They seem to be holding all the cards, but let's put first things first. Let's do what we need to do to stay alive whatever comes, then let's consider all of our other options."

"Thank you," she responded. "What's first?"

"Besides firewood?" I said with a grin.

"Yes, besides firewood," she said with a slight smile.

"First, let's get the cabin ready for a better night's sleep. It's so dusty in there I could barely sleep at all," I said.

"I agree, let's get to it," she said almost with enthusiasm.

On the back porch, I found two old wooden buckets. One would need some patching, but the other would probably hold water. There was a small kettle on the potbellied stove, so I filled both containers at the stream. When I returned, Rebekah was trying to pull the old mattress out the front door. I helped her get it through and stood it up against a nearby tree. With the broad side of the axe, I started pounding it. It produced a considerable dust plume. When the dust finally became significantly less, I pulled off my T-shirt, wetted it, and began to wipe the mattress down. It wasn't ever going to compete with my Sleep Number bed at home, but it had to be better than last night. I left it draping over some bushes as the warm sun applied its healing touch.

Inside, Rebekah was washing down the walls and the cabinets. She had all the kitchen utensils on the front porch, so I began to wash them. There were two cast iron skillets, though one was extremely rusty, the small kettle, one small sauce pan, a Dutch oven, three metal plates, a bowl and a few plastic spoons of various sizes. There was also a kerosene lantern hanging from a peg. It was empty of fuel, but still there were no matches. Furniture-wise, there was a small table with two chairs, the potbellied stove, the bed frame and a rocking chair. That was all. A classic outhouse, with the half-moon cutout in the door, stood off to the side out back, almost leaning up against the cliff face.

In the corner of one cabinet was a tin can without a label, but it seemed to be still safe—at least it wasn't swollen. I refused to look at the expiration date even if it had one. Whatever its contents, it might have to be supper assuming we had to skip breakfast and lunch. On the back porch under a pile of old lumber, I also discovered a five-gallon can half full of kerosene. That would be useful for the lantern. There was also a small barrel that may have been used to hold water, but it, too, was empty except for two dead mice. There was also another rocking chair hanging under the roof, along with a snow shovel.

Back inside, Rebekah had pulled off an old pad that was covering a built-in bench along the wall. She took it out to beat the dust out of it, but I realized that it had been covering a bench seat that when lifted had considerable storage. Inside were two boxes with very little dust. That meant that when closed, it was almost airtight. One box had an assortment of tools, mostly broken and very rusty. There was a newer flashlight, but no batteries. The other box had the remnants of some flour, sugar and a saltshaker. When I moved it, I saw a box of matches, but it only had a dozen or so remaining. It would be very surprising if they would actually light. The matchbox had the silhouette of a lion printed on the cover. Without fully realizing it, the symbol brought to my heart a measure of peace.

Shortly after our lunch without food, and with the tiny cabin almost presentable, we decided to take a break. We walked back behind the cabin, along the small stream towards the falls. We felt good at our progress, but the question of food was looming in our minds. Without saying it, both of us were thinking that we had to at least try to walk out and escape, but that we needed to rest up and be well prepared before trying such an attempt. Without any food supplies, that option on the schedule might have to be moved up on the calendar.

We both walked around the edge of the pool and peered into the depths. Clear water is always deeper than it first appears. If the afternoon sun warms things up, we might have to explore those depths. As we walked into the shadow of the cliff, we both noticed at the same time that several fish darted out from under the ledge we were standing over.

"Maybe those could be supper," we said almost in unison. We both laughed. It was the first laugh from either of us since night before last. Behind the falls there seemed to be a hollow, but a person would get soaked in trying to take a peek. That would have to wait.

Rebekah grabbed my arm and pretended to push me off the ledge towards the deep, but I held my ground. Our entire box canyon was like a private Garden of Eden, but it was our prison. If had we not been standing right beside the falling water, we would have heard it before we did so. There was the throb of a motor. It was a helicopter. We couldn't see it, but it couldn't be far behind the cliff edge, by the sound of it. We both started running back towards the cabin.

The trees and cliff wall kept the chopper hidden until it was pulling away from us. At the tree line along our little lane was a 55-gallon blue barrel. The helicopter must have deposited it. When we unclasped the closure, we opened it to an assortment of items. A quart of peanut butter was the first thing we saw.

"Supper is served," I proclaimed as we both acted like little kids at Christmas. We closed the barrel back up and pushed it over on its side. We took turns rolling it back to the cabin.

Once we really looked inside, we discovered a considerable hoard of food, more than we anticipated. There were the usual staples such as flour and sugar, but there were also a variety of canned goods, snack foods, several heads of cabbage, and a large sack of apples. There was even a box of matches.

As we unloaded the barrel, I began to get very quiet. Rebekah sensed that something was heavy within me and finally asked, "What's the matter?"

It was hard to explain, but I tried, saying, "As we were unloading the food, the gravity of this situation hit me. That's a load of food, because thirty days is a long time. I feel this weight upon my shoulders to protect us, to protect you. I'm scared that I will fail."

"As you told me earlier, we're in this together," she said as she kissed me on the cheek.

"I know we are, and I'm glad of that, but this whole situation has me stumped. As we unloaded the barrel, I realized that our 'friends' thought of everything. They must have a list. This is well planned," I explained.

She shook her head, not understanding what I meant.

So I continued, "They have done this before. That is not the first barrel to be dropped into this canyon.

They know what they're doing. They may have given us all this food, but they're not our friends. We're in their well-crafted and well-thought-out prison."

She didn't respond, contemplating the full implications.

A flag separated the food items from the rest of the stuff in the bottom of the barrel. We assumed that it was an Argentine flag, but it didn't look quite right. Perhaps it was the ranch flag, but we weren't sure. However, we knew what that was for, but didn't voice it. We remembered the threat of raising that flag without the correct information.

At the bottom of the barrel were a set of clean sheets, several towels, two blankets, two pillows and a couple of hand towels. There was also a penknife, and a medium sized hunting knife. It only reinforced what I had just said. They had thought of everything.

The two of us walked the mattress back inside to its place on the frame. It smelled and looked much better than before. The sheets were fitted for a larger bed, but we made them work. With blankets and pillows, it was inviting us for a nap, but we resisted. Supper consisted of canned refried beans and peaches. Fresh meat and anything green was going to be a rarity, but we were thankful. I even said grace at the table before we ate our meal.

"I wonder how Regina is fairing. Do you think they left her at the house?" Rebekah said without really thinking.

"Probably so," I said. "She would be hard to replace. Without us, everything should go back to normal."

"I hope they didn't hurt her any more," Rebekah said, unsure whether she believed if they had or not. She fell asleep stretched out on the newly made bed.

In the tinderbox beside the old stove, I had found several old novels. It appeared that they were being used to start fires one page at a time. From the front covers they looked to be romance westerns, but in Spanish. I grabbed one of them and remembered that I had seen a pencil in the toolbox. I was a list maker, and I needed to start some lists. It's the way I organized my brain, maybe even my soul. The back of the novel had several blank pages.

After moving the rocking chair out to the porch, I starting listing things that I was afraid we might forget. At the top, I wrote, "Essentials, things we would die without."

I started writing as things came to mind:

Food
Water, even when it freezes and snows
Fire and firewood
Shelter—does the roof leak?
Can we stay warm all winter if...?

Then I titled the next page, "Things to consider."

Fresh meat: Fishing, trapping, hunting
    What kind of animals? Weapons?
What varmints may try to get our food?
    Mice, ants, or bigger?

Do we need to ration our food?
Will our supply last 30 days?
Can we make it last longer?
What's around us?
160 miles to main road-East Really?
Box canyon and falls to the West
Canyon walls to the North and South

If we survive the winter-
What will they do then to us?

I need to start praying, but not like a pastor
Like <u>a man who really needs God</u>

What do they think we know about the money?
Does R know more than she has told me?
Would they really kill us?
<u>We must survive</u>!

I tried to erase those last three lines, but the eraser was gone from the pencil, so I unsuccessfully marked them out. With the novel-turned-journal tucked into the stack of wood, I started splitting more firewood. A cooler breeze started coming down the canyon. Within minutes it was much colder. The thought of a dip in the falls was quickly out of the question. It was time for a fire. The old matches worked, and the fire jumped to life in the cast-iron stove. It even started drafting well up the exhaust pipe. It was amazing how a good cleaning and a warm fire changed the atmosphere of the place.

The wind continued, as did the lowering of the temperature. Before it was very dark outside, clouds began to roll in with a light mist. I had moved the rocking chair back inside. I should have gotten the other one down from outside. In our warm cabin retreat, Rebekah came over and sat in my lap. I was glad that I forgotten the other chair. I thought to myself, "I am so glad that I'm not here alone." She seemed to know what I was thinking, or part of it.

CHAPTER 12

Whiteness

The next morning there was a heavy frost but no snow. Several songbirds were letting us know of their presence. I stoked up the stove, and then decided to place our "gift barrel" inside. It seemed to be a new barrel, but I washed and rinsed it out as best I could anyway. Then I started hauling water from the stream. A barrel of water inside would be a good source in the severe cold.

After about the third load, Rebekah was up and stirring. She had no choice. When I came back with the next load, she had breakfast ready. She opened a box of crackers and had retrieved one of the jars of Victoria's amazing strawberry jam. We savored every bite, washing it down with the freshly drawn stream water. The sun eventually found its way into our Garden Paradise, and the frost vanished.

Together we sorted the food items. It appeared to be enough for two for thirty days, but there wasn't a surplus. We needed to be careful. The sacks of beans and rice would go farther than they looked, but the other items could run short.

After we stored it away in the long storage chest, Rebekah said, "There is one major problem that I can see with the food."

"What would that be?" I responded taking her bait.

"I'm not a cook," she said with some force.

I looked her in the face and realized that she wasn't kidding.

"I thought the strawberry jam and crackers were amazing," I countered.

"Lunch is several hours away, and I'm already panicking," she snapped back.

"Wait a minute," I said. "Who said you were in charge of the food? I'm no gourmet, but I can cook. After all, I haven't seen anything in our pantry that looks to be very difficult."

She seemed to relax some.

With that, I reopened the pantry and took out the sack of dried beans. "Would you care to have beans for supper?" I asked.

"Beans for supper sound wonderful," she grinned, "but I've never cooked a bean in my life."

I picked up the freshly cleaned Dutch oven and filled it up to about a third with water. Then I opened the sack of beans, put it into her hands, and helped her pour out several cups. Together we set it on the stovetop, and I said; "Now you can't say that anymore." We both laughed and held each other.

However, as we stood arm in arm, watching the dry beans in the water slowly begin to heat, I realized that her laughter had turned to tears. I pretended to not notice, even though her tears were dripping down my jacket. None of this was going to be easy for either of us, but after a few minutes I resumed my task of filling up the water barrel.

Rebekah walked down to the falls while I continued hauling water. I noticed that she was taking a towel and a change of clothes, but I didn't say a word. The barrel seemed to get bigger with each load. When I finished the last bucket, I decided that I should get the other rocking chair down. When I moved it, I noticed that it was covering up a small door into the attic of the log house. I hadn't noticed it before.

After rinsing off the chair, I stepped up on the kerosene can and opened the attic door. I couldn't see much inside, and to be honest I wasn't sure that I could fit through the tiny opening. I'm not vain, but I didn't want to be caught by Rebekah coming back from her bath wedged in the tiny attic door. Whoever originally made that door was a tad smaller than I was. Looking inside I could see several cracks where daylight was shining. It would have to leak if the wind blew. As I stood there balanced on the kerosene can, I had the same sense that Rebekah had about cooking; I didn't know a thing about repairing roofs.

Suddenly Rebekah asked in a sharp voice, "What's in the attic?" I jumped, nearly falling off the can. I hadn't heard her sneak up behind me. She thought it was humorous, though she really hadn't meant to scare me.

"Did you find thirty-million dollars hidden up there?" she asked with a smirk.

"Yes, a whole pile of money, now we just need to find a grocery store, and maybe an airport," I jousted back. "Actually all I can see are some potential roof leaks," I said.

"That's all?" she kept insisting.

"OK, to be honest, I won't fit through that little door, so I don't know what's up there. You happy?" I barked with just a little bite.

Without a blink in her eye, she said that she thought that she could fit and started to step up on the can.

"Don't go up there," I said, "it's nasty and you just had a bath. You'll get filthy."

She looked down at her clean clothes and said, "You're right; wait just a minute." Without explanation she walked away back towards the thick trees. She wasn't gone long, but when she returned she was wearing her dirty clothes.

She looked at me and said, "Now help me up there. I can't reach it even from that can." She climbed on my back and squeezed through the opening. I was pleased to see that even her small frame found it to be tight. I had made the right decision not to try to force my frame through.

I could hear her searching around, but she didn't say anything. In a moment or two, she handed out a bow with a quiver of arrows. It had been up there for some time, but it might just still be workable. She also tossed out a shovel without a handle, two long boards and a couple of what looked to be saddlebags for a mule.

I helped her back down, and we both started laughing. She was completely covered in dirt and soot.

Her wet hair from her recent bath had changed several shades lighter. Without announcing her plans, she marched off to repeat her bathing. She wasn't upset about getting dirty; instead she was proud of herself.

After stirring the beans, I checked on the bow. It wasn't as old as it first appeared. The string had a few nicks, but it would hold. Once it stretched, it appeared to be in good working order. Three arrows had target points. The other, however, was a hunting point with razor blades, though showing some rust. I dropped one of the target arrows into the notch and pulled. I aimed down the road towards the gate of our private canyon. It shot much farther that I anticipated. I was impressed.

It took me awhile to find the arrow, but I was determined not to lose it. By the time I got back, the newly-bathed Rebekah had the table set, but something else was in the air. She smiled saying, "How do like cornbread and beans?"

"I love cornbread and beans," I said.

She was holding an empty box of cornbread mix as she said. Pointing to the back of the box, "It says that all you add is some water and oil, and bake. We have water, oil and an oven."

The cornbread burned some on the bottom, but soaked in bean juice one could hardly tell. We ate the entire skillet of cornbread and most of the beans. We were too full for dessert, even if we had been offered some.

Before the evening chill, I informed her that it was my turn for a bath. With a clean set of clothes, I headed to the falls. It didn't take me long to discover that the water in the falls was cold enough to give you an instant headache. I was impressed that Rebekah had done this twice. A few seconds was more than enough, but it felt good having done so.

When I returned, I found Rebekah on the front porch studying the back of the Spanish Western that I had left on the woodpile. I hadn't hidden it from her, but I hadn't written it for her either. As she was intently studying it, I was trying to remember what I had written. That's the joy of list making; once you add it to the list, it's out of your crowded mind.

"Those last three lines are interesting, the ones you tried to mark out," she said.

"I can't remember what I said," I responded being somewhat coy.

"The three lines you tried to mark out—they're still readable," she said.

"What do they say?" I asked though my memory was returning.

"They say, let me read it back to you. You said, and I quote: 'Does R know more than she has told me? Would they really kill us? We must survive!" she said with a touch of dramatic flare.

I didn't respond.

"Do you think I know something that I haven't told you?"

I said, "They seem to think you do, but I don't know."

She continued to rock in the old chair as if she was rereading my list. Then she said, "Assuming all goes back to normal for Regina, the house, and whatever business they're in, do you think they will forget about us?"

I shrugged my shoulders. I really didn't know what to say.

"There is something I haven't told you," she said.

"Do I want to know?" I asked.

She wanted me to know anyway. "Before we boarded the charter at Buenos Aires, I called the Boston City Bank. I canceled the automatic bank draft. The $15,000 isn't coming to Box 18 next month. I may have done great harm to Regina. I feel terrible."

"I don't blame you. I probably would have done the same thing," I said, but it did make me wonder why she hadn't told me till now.

"Let's go for a walk. I've got something to show you," I said.

We walked down the lane that led out of the box canyon. The sun was already at the back of the mountains behind us and the sky was on fire. Every step we took we had to stop and turn to see the sunset develop. Eventually we got to the mouth of the canyon with the gate and flagpole. We stood there and looked east across the wide-open Pampas. There really was absolutely nothing that direction. The road that had brought us here just disappeared into the horizon. We both thought without saying it, "160 miles is a long way."

Before we turned around, I pointed to the flagpole and said, "Do you remember what the letter said about raising the flag?"

"Of course, how could I forget? It says they'll come and listen, but that we'll die if we don't have the correct information about the money," she said.

"Yes, that's what it said, but this afternoon when I shot the arrow down here, I got to thinking about that statement. How would they know if the flag is flying? Are they watching us now? If we raise the flag, would they be here tonight, in the morning, or at the end of the month?" I asked.

She said, "I suppose the helicopter will fly by in a month, but I see what you're saying."

"I don't know the answer, but it's a question I've been thinking about. Something doesn't make sense about any of this," I said.

As we walked back towards our cabin in the woods, Rebekah was holding my arm as she said, "I have another question about your list, but if you don't want to answer it's fine."

"Sure, you can ask anything," I responded.

She said, "On your list, you mentioned prayer."

I waited for her to continue.

"I used to pray when my life was wonderful. When all was going well, I had a prayer life, as our pastor used to call it, but when Gary didn't come home, I really started praying, probably for the first time. Night after night I begged God to send him home, but as you know, he never did. After a while I just quit praying."

We continued walking.

As we approached the cabin she added, "When I saw your list, I couldn't help but see that in the middle of the list you said that you were planning to *start* to pray. Had you stopped too?"

I didn't answer until we went inside. It was certainly getting colder, but it didn't feel as cold as it had the other two nights. The cabin was warm, even though the fire was just a bed of coals. We carried in both rocking chairs and sat with our feet on one of the boxes facing the warm stove.

Finally I answered her question, "I think I did stop praying. I loved being a pastor. I loved seeing people 'wake up' into faith, but when Rachel was sick, I started praying with desperation. It was brutal when I tried to preach. I understand now that I had a secret anger towards God. Without realizing it, I just quit praying, and then when I 'retired,' I felt even more abandoned. I was mad at everyone. I was mad at my church for letting me retire. I was mad at myself for retiring. I was mad at my wife for treating me like she did when she was sick. I was mad at the doctors for not finding the cancer early enough. I was even mad at Rachel for dying. I suppose somewhere in all that anger, I just got mad at God, too."

"Wow, we're both a couple of basket cases," she said. For several minutes we let the air clear itself, as if my ugly confession had produced a foul smell.

She broke the silence, "Do you ever pray now?"

"Yes," I said, "I prayed at least three times the day this all began: once at Regina's table, once in the back of the delivery truck and once sitting on the log in front of the falls."

She asked, "What did you pray?"

"At the table, I prayed that they wouldn't take us out and shoot us. In the truck, I prayed for both of us to survive together. On the log, I prayed for wisdom concerning what to do next, but I don't think God was listening at any of the three times."

She grabbed my hand, looked me in the face, and said, "Why do you say that?"

I looked in her eyes, but I didn't know what to say. She was very serious.

Then she continued, "It looks to me like he answered you every time, but of course, I'm not a preacher like you are. They didn't shoot us. We both survived together, at least so far, and you knew the next morning to start cutting firewood. It looked to me like he answered all three of your prayers."

I continued rocking. Tears started running down my face. For the first time I tasted real hope. I knew that whatever was to happen, we both would survive and even flourish. An assurance moved into my heart, but all I said was, "Thanks. I needed to hear that."

Before bedtime, I stepped outside to bring in some firewood for the night. Two things I immediately noticed. One, it was much colder now, and two, it wasn't very dark out, but it took me a second or two to realize why. It was snowing. I stepped back inside and invited Rebekah to come join me on the porch. We stood there for a moment in the absolute silence and just watched the big flakes fall from above. It was hard to describe why, but those few moments on the porch watching the snow was one of the most special times of my life.

CHAPTER 13

It is Well Isn't It?

I slipped out early the next morning. I didn't have any specific plans, but I grabbed the bow and quiver of arrows. There were several inches of snow covering almost everything, but the clouds had already passed over and the morning sky showed the beauty of the stars. The quick walk along the lane towards the front gate was invigorating, breathing in the cold air. As I reached the gate, I spotted the tracks of a small animal. I wasn't sure, but my guess was that is was a rabbit. Another few steps confirmed my guess. A large rabbit was standing about thirty yards in front of me. His long ears were on alert trying to determine what I was.

After easing one of the target points into place, I quietly pulled the bow back. At that distance I expected a few inches of drop, so I aimed just above the top of his ears. It felt good to hear the arrow slice through the morning air, but it passed right between the rabbit's ears without touching fur. I was impressed with my shooting ability, but still walked away meatless. The arrow disappeared into the snow-covered grass and was nowhere to be found. I marked the area so that once the snow melted I could return to retrieve it.

I decided to keep walking out onto the Pampas' prairie. In another hundred yards, I saw deer tracks. I assumed that the mountains had deer of some sort, and probably many other animals. It might be worth sitting out on another morning to watch. The longer I walked east, the more I started looking south. It appeared that several miles down to the south there was an opening to another canyon, perhaps much like ours. That would be worth investigating as well, but the distance was hard to judge.

When I got back to the cabin, Rebekah was sitting on the porch wrapped in one of the blankets. She too loved the snow, and waved when I appeared. She yelled, "How is my great white hunter?"

"Still hungry," I yelled back. I decided not to mention the rabbit. She probably wouldn't have appreciated the skill it takes to shoot an arrow between a rabbit's ears.

Sitting beside her on the bench, she snuggled up beside me and asked what was the order for the day. I started to report on the possible canyon several miles south, but decided that could wait as well.

"Perhaps I should check my list to see what we should do today," I said with some jest. She faked a punch to my chin to retaliate.

"In case you haven't checked your calendar, today is Sunday. Maybe we should go to church. You could even preach me a sermon," she said.

I faked a punch to her chin.

"No, I'm serious, Richard," she countered. Then she took my hand, and without another word we started down the snow covered path towards the falls. When we arrived, she spread the blanket she had been wrapped with and draped it over the dead log after I brushed off the snow. We both had a seat.

She began, "The way I see our situation is like this. We've both been robbed and deeply wounded, you by cancer, and I by these criminals. Yet it appears to me that we both have a choice to make, a choice that will determine the kind of persons we'll be the rest of our lives, however long that is."

She paused for a moment as the bright sun reflected off the waterfall. Almost as if on cue, a chunk of snow slid from the cliff above into the pool below. The splash served to emphasize her words.

"I don't know what really happened to Gary, and I still don't know what he was involved with, but my heart now says he's gone. My mind has said this for several years. Even if he's sitting in some cabin like we are, he left me. He chose to live a life without me. He had his own house, his own country, his own fishing adventures, and even his own damned Easter dinner. None of it involved me, absolutely none of it," she said, pausing to catch her breath. For a Boston woman it was quite a lengthy statement.

But she continued, "To be honest, until a couple of weeks ago, I was content to remain bitter, angry and alone. But that week of fly fishing with you sparked something within me. I don't want to be that person anymore. I had no choice in what happened to Gary, but I do have a choice concerning what happens to me. You and I may not get out of this alive, but even if we don't, my soul is going to be right with the Father. Does that make any sense at all?"

It was my turn. "That may be the best sermon I've ever heard, and I agree. Life tumbled in on me and almost buried me. Before we discovered that Rachel had cancer, she turned mean. Her personality switched over like Mr. Hyde. She suddenly hated me.

"She said things to our friends and daughters that were terrible. She attacked me as a spouse, as a father and as a pastor. I had no defense. She cost me everything. Several times I almost pulled a Gary. I just wanted to disappear. Then when we discovered the cancer, I felt guilty and horribly full of shame. At the funeral I said some things to God, things that I wish I hadn't said."

Rebekah took my hand and held it without speaking.

I continued, "I thought I was finished with the Father, but really I thought He was finished with me. The week of fly-fishing with you made me rethink who I was, or at least what I was becoming. Then last night...you challenged me. As we stood there and watched the snowfall, I felt the Father hug me. It was almost more than I could take. I didn't say anything, but standing there last night with you, and with Him, was one of the most intimate moments in my life.

"When we crawled into bed last night and went to our separate corners, I just laid there, knowing without a doubt that He loves me. If this is where my life ends, then well...then, it's well with my soul."

Still holding hands, she said, "That sounds like a hymn we used to sing at my church in Boston."

In the silence of the snow-covered canyon, we united our voices and sang softly the old hymn that we both knew:

When peace, like a river, attendeth my way,
When sorrows like sea billows roll,
Whatever my lot,
Thou has taught me to say,
It is well; it is well...with my soul.

A small flock of yellow-bellied songbirds flew down the falls chirping and singing. Unaware of our presence, they flapped and fluttered in the snow along the riverbank. We both remained perfectly still. It was like a special gift on a day that had already contained many special gifts.

After "church," I decided to split some more firewood. Rebekah helped stack it. We refilled the front porch, and then started on the back. By midafternoon the snow had melted, except in a few shady areas. The warm Pampas wind was blowing up the canyon and the cold air was flushed out. In the warmth we decided to go visit the falls together. If we put on our dirty clothes, and stood under the water it would be like a washing machine. I think Rebekah's clothes got cleaner than mine, because she could stand under the falls longer than I. The water was too cold for me to stay very long.

We discovered that there was indeed a little cave behind the falls. It wasn't very large, but we could stand in it and not have the water splash us. At first it was too dim to really see much, but eventually our eyes adjusted. In the very back there were some drawings—pictures of hands, left hands to be precise. I told Rebekah that not far from the house near Bajo Los Caracoles was a UNISCO site. I couldn't remember the name of it, but Victoria had told us about it. I read that it dated back almost 10,000 years. It too contained mostly the outlines of left hands. We studied the drawings as best as we could in the dim light, but it didn't make much sense, other than somebody wanted us to know that they had been there, too.

I stepped out from the falls on the opposite side from which we entered. As I was drying off in the warm sun, I noticed that in front of me, about eye level, was a stone in the rock wall that didn't match the colors of the other rock. It seemed to be a different type of rock, and the moss wasn't as thick on it as elsewhere.

When I examined it, I discovered that it was loose. It easily rolled out when I pushed on it from the bottom. In its place was a perfect little cove. There was nothing in it, but it was odd how it fit. I put it back, and finished getting dressed and joined Rebekah back in the cabin. For supper we opened a can of corned beef hash and peas. Neither of us was fond of green peas from a can, but mixed with the hash we ate the whole can. There were hardly ever any leftovers after our meals. As we prepared for the early darkness of our canyon, I started studying the rock cliff that was nearest our cabin. There weren't any odd colored rocks or hollowed out coves that I could see. Why was there one by the falls? Suddenly I had an idea.

While Rebekah was trying to read one of the Spanish novels, I walked back up to the falls before darkness fell. From farther back, I could see the cliff better than I could directly under it. If I hadn't have seen it earlier, I wouldn't have seen it then, but I knew what I was looking for. I was right. There were other hidden coves up above the one I discovered. It was a rock ladder. I suspected that it climbed all the way up the cliff.

I didn't tell Rebekah about my discovery. I wanted to wait and surprise her in the morning, and after all, the ancient steps may not go all the way up and out. Who knows whether it might crumble, and even if it were a way out, where would it go from there?

As darkness recaptured our private canyon, we positioned our rocking chairs before the stove. The box served again as our footstool for our feet, nestled together. Once we were settled, Rebekah started the conversation.

"If none of this had happened, what would we be doing tonight?" she asked.

"Do you mean if we hadn't come back to Argentina and I was in Lexington and you were in Boston, what would we do doing?"

"Yes," she answered.

"I know what I would be doing," I said.

"Really? What would you be doing tonight? Watching Kentucky basketball?"

"Maybe, but even if I was watching the Wildcats beat the stuffing out of somebody, I would be thinking about you," I said.

"You're teasing me. By now you would have forgotten me. You didn't even call me when you got home to Lexington."

"I texted you when I thought you would have gotten home. I didn't want to scare you away. I was afraid that if I sounded too...aggressive, that I might mess things up, but you didn't respond to my text," I countered.

"I know. I saw it a few minutes after I looked under Gary's chair. My world was spinning in circles by then. I'm sorry." She paused for several minutes.

"So if you were home in Lexington tonight, you would be thinking about me?" she said.

"I hope that feeling might go both ways," I said. "Besides, if I wasn't at home in Lexington thinking about you, then I might be in Boston seeing you."

She asked, "What did you think when I called you the next day?"

"At first I didn't think it was you. It didn't sound like you. I thought maybe you were having a friend call me to tell me to never call again, and then when I realized it really was you, I didn't know what to think. I could tell you were hurting," I said.

"Did you consider not coming to Boston? That was a big request," she said.

"I was certainly confused, but it never crossed my mind not to catch the earliest flight out."

"My, my, you were smitten weren't you?" she answered.

"Yes, yes, I was, and yes, I am," I said squeezing her hand a touch tighter.

"Not me," she said, "I'm just now starting to like you a tiny bit."

"You're a liar," I said with a smile. She squeezed my hand even tighter.

It's odd but the first morning at the cabin, I filled and tested the kerosene lantern after finding the can of fuel on the back porch. After some cleaning and adjusting, it worked fairly well, but since that time we hadn't used it. The glow and flicker of the stove had been all we needed or wanted.

CHAPTER 14

Ancient Stairs

The next morning we both hiked back to the falls when it was barely daylight. I popped out the odd colored stone and showed Rebekah the niche that appeared to be cut out from the cliff, and, sure enough, another one was cut and hidden just about where the next foot would need to land. As I climbed, Rebekah spotted where each of the footholds might be. She could see them from farther away than I could up close. Not being fond of heights, I could feel my body tighten in its nervousness, but the cliff was at a slight slope so that with my feet anchored, my torso was touching the rock. At about forty feet up, at what appeared to be over halfway, the camouflaged footholds disappeared. She couldn't see any more and I couldn't feel any.

Just as I was about to start back down, I noticed an odd stone off to my left. The hidden steps were turning sideways. After discovering several footholds

127

horizontal, I could see a crack in the wall itself. From below, it was completely hidden.

It was a relief to know that I could actually squeeze through the crack, though it barely accommodated me. That would have been even more embarrassing than the attic door. Through the crack was a passageway into a small cave. At the back of the cave was another crack with clearly defined steps. They were clearly manmade. From Rebekah's point of view, I just disappeared behind a rock. She kept watching, and even yelled a couple of times, but I was gone. I followed the steps up to another level, which finally deposited me at the top overlooking the canyon. Walking over to the edge, I waved at a concerned Rebekah. She looked greatly relieved as she waved back.

The stream flowing into our paradise appeared not as impressive above as it did cascading over the falls, but about fifty feet upstream over bedrock, there was another deep pool and a smaller falls. I was up there so I had to explore, but before I disappeared over the edge, I heard a yell from below. I couldn't hear what she was saying over the roar of the falls, but it was evident from her hand motions that she desired to climb the rock face as well. At first I tried to warn her not to come, but she wasn't taking my hints. If I could make it, she could make it. I climbed back down the steps in the crack to the upper cave to wait for her to scale the wall.

As I watched her negotiate the footholds, I admitted what I had already realized. These "foothold stairs" were remnants of an ancient people that used this arroyo many years before it became part of the ranch, or even our prison. Whether they led us to actual freedom or not wasn't the question; they had already given us a feeling of freedom, and for that I was thankful.

It didn't take her long before she was squeezing into the crack beside me. Seeing her dancing eyes made me wonder why in the world I tried to dissuade her from coming up to join me. I led her up the back steps and onto to the upper level. It was almost level over to the pool and smaller falls. There were numerous boulders scattered around obviously having fallen from above. The next level wasn't difficult to climb at all, and once up there we discovered that it was considerably larger. Our small stream was skipping from hole to hole across the rocky terrain, but it was easy for us to continue climbing beside it.

Across the wide-open rocky bench, we could see another tall cliff blocking our advance. The closer we became, the taller it appeared. We stayed as close as we could to the stream, and picked our way through the boulders. In front of us there appeared to be a round natural amphitheater cut into the cliff. Dark stripes of water stains were decorating the back of the formation. Several cliff birds were performing acrobatics in the updraft caused by the amphitheater. It was clearly a naturally-formed cut, but in the bottom were several small stone structures. They reminded me of the Anasazi ruins of the American Southwest. It wasn't a full city, as in Mesa Verde or Chaco Canyon, but there were at least four stone structures in various degrees of decay. As I stepped back to admire the ruins, I realized that I was standing on the edge of a square-cut pit, probably an old house. Once we noticed the pattern and began looking, we spotted a dozen or more other caved-in pit houses.

Our stream turned back to the south and ran along the edge of the cliff face. We decided to press on just to see what we could see. About a mile or so along the base of the cliff, another falls came down in four sections. The mist was creating a rainbow, but that was the end of us following the stream. There seemed to be no way above the steep cliffs. In another mile or so, it appeared to us that a small canyon was forming below us, very similar to our own canyon. We walked up as close as we could to the edge, and could see the same type of big trees as were in our canyon, but we could see no cabin or road.

It was time for a breather, so we found one of many flat rocks to rest ourselves. The view down the cliffs into the Pampas region was spectacular. You could see beyond forever. Rebekah claimed that she could see the ocean, but I argued that it had to be at least five hundred miles; however, she still insisted. Maybe she was right.

A black-chested eagle floated overhead on the wind currents. It was the same kind of eagle we had seen while fishing two weeks ago. It never flapped its wings the entire time it was in our view. It just floated in its pure freedom.

"To be hostages in a personal prison, we're doing fairly good for ourselves," Rebekah said. She meant it to be light-hearted, but it served to bring both of us down to reality.

We were prisoners, captives and hostages. We weren't sure how to define our situation, but yes, it was a well-decorated prison, and we weren't exactly suffering.

She asked, "What do you think we should do?"

"Let's just sit here a little longer," I answered.

"No, that's not what I meant. What do you think we should do before winter? Should we try to walk the hundred and sixty miles? Should we try to hike out a different direction? Should we try to spend the winter in the cabin?"

"What are you thinking?" I responded.

After a few moments of thought, she responded, "I trust you. I will do whatever you think we should do, but please, whatever we do, let's do it together. Don't leave me. Don't try to walk out without me, promise me."

"I'm not sure what we should do, but I promise, I will not leave you alone, okay?" I said.

"By the way, I noticed something," she said.

I said, "What's that?"

"I noticed that you're not wearing your wedding ring," she said with a smile.

"Neither are you," I bounced back.

"I guess we're both single," she said.

I leaned over and kissed her. Though we had been together almost every minute, day and night for nearly a week, we had hardly kissed since we were standing on Regina's deck. Even though we were sharing a bed in the cabin because we had little choice, we were both very careful. We cared too much for each other to allow things to get uncomfortable. In the back of both of our minds was the promise about "times and seasons." We strolled back to the exit steps leading down into our arroyo. We had explored farther than we realized, and it took us longer than we expected. In truth, had it not been for our stream it would have been easy to walk right past the entrance to our stone ladder.

I was somewhat nervous about going down the stair steps, but Rebekah decided she wanted to go first. The only treacherous section was the fifteen feet we had to slide over horizontally, but she made it easily. While I was waiting for her to complete the descent, I explored the little cave. There was a raised pile of stones in one corner that looked to be almost stacked. I kicked them over without really thinking, and saw something. It was a plastic bag with a small notebook inside. It appeared in the dim light to match the fishing journal I discovered in Gary's fishing vest, but thumbing through it I could tell that it had been used for a different purpose. I slipped it in my pocket, and began my descent. I didn't mention the find after I completed the climb down. I wasn't sure what it contained, if anything.

We cooked the cabbage and another pan of cornbread. After we had eaten every bite, Rebekah informed me that she didn't think she liked cabbage, but that her opinion had changed. While she was moving our rocking chairs back to their positions in front of the stove, I retrieved the fishing journal that I found in Gary's fishing vest from my bag. I had forgotten about it with all that had happened, and thus had failed to mention it to Rebekah. I also lit the lantern and hung it from its hook in the ceiling. She looked at me with a question, but I didn't explain.

As our feet took their positions on the single box before the stove, I produced the first journal and explained to her where it came from. The lantern was dimmer than I thought it would be, and she was having a difficult time reading, so I moved the lantern down to the box so she could get closer to the light. She thumbed through it, but made very few comments.

When she seemed satisfied, she said, "His fishing life without me was very extensive. I still don't understand. Perhaps I never will."

I then produced the other journal and explained where I found it. I hadn't read it yet, but I felt like it might be more than a fishing journal. I handed it to her, and she bent over to allow the lantern to illumine the first page. She flipped through it and confirmed that it was signed, "Gary Black." She thumbed back to the front and read it out loud in its entirety.

These are the thoughts, prayers and confessions of Gary Black:

I'm convinced that my days on this earth are but few. I have gotten myself into a web with no way out. It will cost me both my life and soul. I believed in the beginning, that the "business" we are involved with was for the good of many. We provided transportation for various indigenous persons to families that would give them a chance at new and better lives. It was very lucrative, and I was the principal accountant and money handler.

Perhaps I should have realized the ugly nature of our business before I did so, but I didn't, to my shame, and even when I did smell something nasty, I failed to do anything. The guilt has forever stained my soul.

Eventually I understood the various levels of horror we were perpetuating through our "business," but by then I was already in too deep. I discovered that most of our "clients," were being sold as European and Middle Eastern sex slaves. When I quizzed G and the others, they warned me to keep silent. When I pressured them, I saw the true nature of my business associates and the danger of big money. They threatened that my wife would be taken and sold if I did not maintain the status quo.

Under such a threat, I made the hardest decision I've ever made. I died to my wife without a single explanation. I have felt more shame in that decision than even the filth of our disgusting export business.

My last scheme was an attempt to preserve my own life. As the business accountant, I embezzled a sizable sum from our business funds. I have hidden those funds in a secret place. I assumed that as long as the money wasn't discovered, that I would be protected. I underestimated their anger and miscalculated their response. Now I am isolated in this canyon. I believe that in the next few days my associates plan to dispose of me forever.

This is my confession. I doubt that anyone will ever find it, and I know that I am beyond redemption in God's eyes. I wish, with all my heart, that I had listened to my wonderful Rebekah. She sensed the danger, but I refused to listen. Whatever comes my way, I deserve it, and worse, but for what it's worth now, I'm sorry. I am so sorry.

Signed, Gary Black

"This is the cabin where Gary stayed. This is his canyon," she said. I couldn't tell if there were tears on her cheek, but I suspected there were.

"He sat right here in front of this fire writing these words," she said. "He may have died right here on this floor," she added.

She glanced through the rest of the journal, but saw no other entry. We rocked for several minutes before the warm and comforting fire, but no other words were spoken. Then suddenly she stood and stepped over to the bed and crawled under the covers. I continued sitting before the fire until the wee hours of the morning.

Now we knew the extent of their ugly business. I had quietly assumed that it was probably illegal drugs. I never considered sex trafficking. That was a tough confession to read from your own spouse. In my memory, I walked through the pages of the ledger we found in the safe at Regina's. The sheer number of entries was staggering, and that just reflected three years. This was a well-oiled business to operate with that kind of volume.

They were professional slavers. What will that mean for me? What will that mean for us? As I pondered our futures, I thought to myself, *I may never sleep again.* I was glad Rebekah could.

CHAPTER 15

Storms

The next morning I decided to split more firewood. We probably had enough for several months, but I needed the physical activity. I thought about taking the bow and arrows down the canyon and perhaps wait for a deer or rabbit, but I didn't want to be gone when Rebekah awakened. Last night's reading material was difficult to listen to, even from my perspective. I wanted to be near in case she needed me. It was much warmer than it had been on most mornings. An east wind was blowing up the canyon. As a kid back in West Texas, an east wind usually meant moisture from the Gulf. I wondered what it meant here on the eastern side of the Andes.

"Do you want some breakfast?" she asked. She was standing on the porch wrapped in one of the blankets. I hadn't noticed the door open.

"Sure," I said, "what's on the menu?"

"You're going to laugh, but I woke up this morning thinking about pancakes," she said.

"Pancakes?" I said while just standing and holding the old axe. "That's sounds great. Let's cook some pancakes."

I had never made pancakes from scratch before, but I thought I knew most of the essentials. We had flour, sugar, oil, evaporated milk, and baking powder. There were even some freeze-dried eggs. We didn't have any butter, or syrup, but I had an idea for that.

We mixed up the batter until it looked to be about right. Then I poured a cup of sugar with a cup of water and put it on the stove. Then I added a tablespoon of the strawberry jam that was still left and added that to the pan. Rebekah stirred the concoction as the skillet heated. The first pancake fell apart, but that happens on every first batch of pancakes. The next few browned perfectly, while the strawberry syrup came to a boil. We each had a stack of three drenched in the red brew. We both were impressed as we licked our plates clean.

As we cleaned up our cooking mess, she said, "I think we need to seriously consider what we're going to do."

As I wiped down the cast iron, I nodded, but inside I really didn't have a clue. Our lives in the canyon were perfect. We had all we needed. That could change in a heartbeat when or if our hosts showed back up, but until then we didn't have to make a decision.

Gary's journal confirmed to me that they were indeed "*medios,*" as Regina had said several times, but "mean" was an understatement. I wonder if Regina knew what their business really involved?

"We've been here five days. I think that we have done well, but if we are going to try to walk out, then we better do it sooner than later. Once the serious winter storms strike, our options may be severely limited. What are you thinking?" I asked.

"I think they assume that we will not survive the winter, but if we do, they will kill us anyway. I believe that we need to do something, but I'm not sure what it is," she replied.

I spent the rest of the morning hauling more water to our indoor barrel. I started cooking some rice and beans and inspected the roof again from the outside. It appeared that most of the visible cracks were wooden shingles that had twisted. By realigning them and tacking them back in place, most of the gaps seemed to close, but a big rain with wind would create leaks no matter what we did.

While I was on the roof, I started studying the cliff overhead. There appeared to be a large boulder almost directly over our outhouse, and it appeared to barely be perched on the edge. That wouldn't be a pleasant experience if it were to give way. That afternoon I explained to Rebekah that I was planning to climb the rock steps at the falls, and then walk the edge of the canyon just to check things out from above. I didn't tell her about my fear of the boulder. She agreed and decided to let me go alone, if I agreed to yell at her once I was above the cabin.

It didn't take me long to make the climb to the cave and then onto the next level. I even stopped and inspected the pile of rocks where I discovered Gary's journal, but I found nothing else of interest. Our little canyon was amazing from above. The pool at the falls was perfectly clear looking down from the cliff top. I could even see the fish that we had yet to try to catch. The trees of the canyon were tall, but none of them quite reached the top of the cliffs. I noticed several bird nests high up that we hadn't seen from below.

The tree that stood over our "church pew" log at the end of the meadow may have been the largest of any of the trees in the canyon. As I admired it, I noticed something wedged in a fork of the limbs about 20 feet up. I was too far to identify what it was, but it appeared to be round and about the size of a soda can. It was interesting in its location, but I passed it off. When I climbed down to the ledge over the cabin, I could see Rebekah in front of the cabin waiting for me. We waved at each other. She really was an amazing individual. We had to get out of this mess alive. We simply had to. Watching her wave and smile from below, I became even more committed to finding a way out of this trap.

The boulder that appeared to be perched over our outhouse was much bigger than it appeared to be from below. It was firmly attached into the wall, and didn't seem to be going anywhere anytime soon. Even if it was about to fall, it was of such size that I couldn't budge it. However, as I inspected the boulder from all sides, I noticed a small square of glass on the side of one stone near the base of the boulder. I tried to pick it up, but I found that it was actually mounted to the stone. When I picked up the stone, I discovered that it was wired to another can, like the one I noticed in the fork of the tree.

A close examination confirmed my first impression. It was a tiny camera pointing down at the cabin. The glass was a small solar panel used to power it. There was a tiny antenna to broadcast the signal. We were being watched. We were on film. That's how they would know if the flag had been raised. I wondered how many more cameras were watching us. I carefully replaced the stone that protected the camera. I hoped that whoever was watching hadn't seen me discover their "eye."

I walked on down the edge of the canyon towards the gate, and discovered one more stone pile that was sheltering another solar-powered camera. Though our cabin and canyon had a Garden of Eden feel, now I knew that it also had the "crafty creature" slithering around. We had discovered that God was with us, but now we knew that evil wasn't far away either.

After walking the loop, I returned to the cabin feeling violated. I found myself looking up into every tree and studying every rock of the cliff face. I didn't discover any more of the photographic devices, but my imagination believed that they were everywhere.

After I explained to Rebekah what I discovered, she didn't have the same reaction. She seemed to have already assumed that we were being watched. To confirm that suspicion didn't change anything for her, but as she walked towards the outhouse, I felt uneasy and I tried to warn her, "These perverts may have cameras everywhere," but she didn't appear worried.

That evening in our rocking chairs before the stove, I explained to her that I was ready to do something.

I couldn't just stay here and wait for the snows. I felt like a fish in a kid's aquarium, just waiting for disaster to fall. When she asked what I was proposing, I didn't have an answer. I just knew that we had to decide something. I really wanted to stay the month and watch for the helicopter. Which direction would it come from? How far would it have traveled? However, waiting to the end of the month no longer seemed like a possibility. The winter snows could set in by then.

"Those small cameras...the antennae are tiny. I might be wrong, but I don't see how those things can be sending a signal very far," I said.

She asked, "What are you saying?"

"I'm thinking that before we start walking a hundred and sixty miles, that we might need to explore our area another few days or so," I said.

She nodded and said, "I'm game. Let's start tomorrow. Which direction do you propose we start investigating?"

"I don't have a clue," I said.

She said with firmness, "Why don't we pray about it?"

When I looked in her face, I realized that she wasn't kidding. She really wanted us to pray. Why not? Did I believe that God *could* help us or not? Did I believe that God *wanted* to help us or not?

I took her hand and prayed, "Lord, we need guidance. Show us what to do, when to do it and how to do it. Protect us..." I wasn't sure what else to pray so I just stopped.

Rebekah took over. She prayed picking up where I left off, "Lord, protect us from evil. Give Richard peace that you're with us, and that you'll guide our steps. Lord, I love this man, and I beg you to lead him as he leads us, Amen."

"Amen," I added. I loved her too, but I didn't say it. We sat in silence the rest of the evening, as the coals slowly grew dimmer and dimmer.

We fell asleep in our rocking chairs with our feet intertwined on the box, but suddenly we were awakened. A lightning bolt struck with the clap of thunder following almost immediately. We both stood straight up. Another flash came, and then another. We stepped out on the porch, but it wasn't raining...yet. It was perfectly still. Not a leaf was moving, but that changed in seconds.

It started with a brisk wind, then a smattering of rain, and then sleet. We lit the lantern and stoked the fire as the powerful thunderstorm set in upon us. There were a couple of small drips in the ceiling so we placed pans to catch the water, but overall the roof was holding tight. For at least an hour the lightning storm raged, but as it moved away the steady rain continued. It was pouring torrents of water. I kept peering upwards, checking the roof, and from time to time checking outside.

I could hear our little stream now raging through the trees, but it was too dark to tell how much it had risen. The cabin was higher than the stream, but how much higher? I really hadn't thought about it till now. Eventually the torrential rain settled down, leaving a slow and steady tapping on the wooden shingles. After emptying our drip-catching pots, we went on to bed. Rebekah snuggled up beside me. It was the first time we had even touched while laying in bed, except of course the first night before we had sheets and blankets.

With the rain continuing, she whispered in my ear, "I wish we were married." Then she rolled over and moved to her side.

I lay there on my back still feeling the warmth of her body where she had been snuggling. Most of the world, and all of Hollywood, would assume that since we were sleeping together, that we were doing more than just "sleeping" together; yet I wondered if anyone really understood. It wasn't about being moral or chaste, and it wasn't that I felt that God would be angry. This woman was too valuable to take advantage. Even as her body warmth dissipated, I knew that I loved her. I loved her more than life itself.

Before it was light enough to see, I was up and outside. The clouds were gone, but our personal stream had risen to become a mighty river. Its bank was at the very corner of the cabin; if it had been much higher, we might have had serious problems. Some of the firewood that I had split, but not yet stacked, had washed down towards the gate, scattering through the grass. After sliding on my boots I started walking down the lane. The stream spread out in multiple channels as it reached the mouth of the canyon. It was truly amazing how much water was flowing into the prairie grass. This was the kind of rain that would certainly mess up a fly fishing trip. As I walked back towards the cabin, I resisted the urge to wave at the cameras.

We relaxed most of the day as the waters slowly receded. By midafternoon our stream was back to normal size and almost clear. As I explored the stream up to the falls, I noticed movement in one of the small pools. A fat, healthy trout was stranded, unable to swim back upstream to the waterfall hole. It didn't take long for the fisherman in me to pounce on supper. He was a 14-inch brookie with beautiful colors: bright orange fins with blue speckles. We decided to bake him with salt and pepper. Served over a bed of rice, diced canned tomatoes and peaches, the trout was tasty. We felt blessed, indeed. I caught Rebekah licking the last drops of the peach syrup from the can when she thought I wasn't watching. We laughed and hugged, and then laughed some more.

The next morning, assuming the weather allowed, we planned to start exploring in a wider circle. We needed to decide which way we should attempt to escape our personal Garden of Eden.

CHAPTER 16

Exploring the Neighborhood

The rock felt secure, but as my weight leaned against it, I could feel it shift. I couldn't hold myself onto the cliff much longer. I was sliding backwards, and then I began to tumble over and over. I plummeted off the edge of the cliff. I was falling into a wide-open space. All I could do was scream—

"Richard! *Richard!*" Rebekah was shaking me, attempting to rouse me from my restless slumber. Eventually, I sorted through which was real and which was my dream world.

Seeing Rebekah's face brought me to consciousness, but my heart was still racing. My scream had been so loud that I had startled her from her sleep. She thought that a bear was dragging me outside, but in reality I was just falling off a mountain. Our plan was to leave the cabin before daylight so that their hidden cameras couldn't spot us. We had only found the three cameras, but we assumed that there were others. We fired up the potbellied stove so that a smoke plume would be visible most of the morning.

Last night I had packed the old saddlebags Rebekah found in the attic. We packed enough supplies to be out overnight, but we weren't planning to pursue anything beyond that. Our goal was to locate a viable target. I carried the bags over my shoulders. Rebekah was wearing one of our blankets. I slit a hole in the blanket for her head so she could wear it like a *serape*. Negotiating the rock steps in the dark wasn't as easy as we had contemplated, but inching up slowly by feel we both eased into the hidden cave without incident. With nothing but the stars, we stood on top looking down into our dark garden paradise.

In our first exploration at this upper level, we went south. We had reached the beginning of a similar canyon to ours, but we hadn't seen any sign of life. More importantly when we had looked down the mouth of the neighboring canyon, there was no sign of a road. So our choices seemed to be to continue south again past the one canyon we had already seen, or to explore to the North. We took turns looking at the two possibilities. The eastern sky was starting to lighten up just slightly.

"Which way are you thinking?" Rebekah asked.

I responded, "North, I think, just because we haven't explored that direction at all. What do you think?"

"South," she said.

"Really? Any reason?" I asked.

"Because you said south," she said.

"I don't remember saying south," I retorted.

"Less than an hour ago, when you were dreaming, before you fell of the cliff, you shouted at the top of your voice, 'South!'" she said.

"You're kidding, right?" I asked.

She responded, "Nope, that's what you said, but what you meant by it I'm not sure. We did ask God to give us some insight, didn't we? Why wouldn't your scream be an answered prayer?"

I nodded in agreement and said, "Then let's go south, but wait, let's call 911 first." I pulled out my cell phone and turned it on. It still had power, but there was no signal. However, I pretended that a call was going through: "Yes, is this the 911 dispatch? It is? I'm Richard Dempsey. I'm a prisoner here in the Andes with the most beautiful woman in the world...why is that a prison you ask?"

Rebekah pushed me away and told me that I had a warped sense of humor, but she laughed. By now the sky had grown even lighter, so we started our trek south. Rebekah led the way, styled up wearing her blue quilted serape and fishing cap. She started at a fairly good pace, and we arrived at the mouth of the next canyon sooner than we anticipated. We even paused a moment on the flat rock where Rebekah was sure she could see the ocean, and where we both noticed that neither of us were wearing our wedding rings.

Our speed increased as the morning sun illuminated and warmed us. We were on no schedule, but in the back of my head I was thinking that whichever direction we pursued, that we would walk only till midafternoon depending upon the weather. Neither of us knew what we were looking for exactly, but we were certainly on a mission. We walked through lunchtime without discussing food. That's not entirely true. We didn't discuss stopping to eat, but we did discuss favorite restaurants and menus. We outlined with detail the meals we would order the day this would all be behind us.

I was craving a salad bar piled high with fresh vegetables, followed by a perfectly grilled sirloin. Rebekah confessed that she was craving a chicken teriyaki burrito from Boloco's in Boston, but that she would be embarrassed for anyone to know that she had ever even been in a Boloco's.

Rebekah also talked about what it was like to live in Boston. She outlined how Bostonites seemed unfriendly to outsiders, but in actuality, they were extremely unfriendly. That made me laugh. She explained that Bostonites considered themselves in a higher class than anyone else, and were increasingly judgmental based upon the distance you lived from downtown Boston. She explained that her business often took her into the homes of the Boston wealthy, both the old money and nouveau rich. In such situations, she hid the fact that she had been raised in a small town in Indiana and only came to Boston to attend school. Such details would not have been good for business.

My watch said that we had been walking over six hours. In front of us was a slight rise blocking our view. I decided that once we climbed over it and could see what was in front of us that we would need to think about what our next step would be. I didn't voice that, but we had been walking fast. As we climbed to the top of the rise, we both could see a canyon opening in front of us. There was another stream coming in from the south. There had to be a waterfall as it poured into the canyon. Judging from the size of the stream, it would be a bigger falls than ours.

I sensed that we needed to be careful. I wasn't sure why, but I suggested that we both get down low and peer over the edge just in case. There was probably nothing to be seen and nothing to see us, but it felt right to at least be careful. When we eased up on the side of a boulder on the edge, we could glimpse down into the canyon. It was wider than ours, and thick with trees. We couldn't see the falls, but we could hear it. There was nothing else to be seen.

"This cliff appears to be straight down to the bottom. I don't think we should assume that there is a hidden rock ladder. I think we should walk along the top edge and explore it from above. Even if we find nothing, it will dump us out on the Pampas and maybe we can return to the Garden of Eden from below. Does that work for you?" I offered. She nodded in agreement. We both knew that we would not be returning to our cozy cabin until sometime tomorrow.

About two hundred yards along the edge, we got a glimpse of the stream below as it meandered through the trees. We did notice that the trees in this canyon seemed to be taking on the beginning phases of their fall colors. They certainly appeared to be more yellow with a touch of orange than the trees in our canyon.

As I was pointing that observation out to Rebekah, I noticed something through the trees. Another step or two opened my view briefly. It was what I thought.

There was a walking trail. It was on the other side of the stream from where we stood, and was mostly hidden in the tall grass, but for a few feet looking down from our angle, it was definitely a foot trail, well traveled. In our canyon, the path from the cabin to the falls was barely visible even while walking it. It didn't have much traffic. This trail appeared to be much better traveled. That meant that this canyon was used more than ours. Instinctively we both backed farther away and ducked down even more.

Without saying anything we continued down the gentle ridge. The canyon was becoming narrower in front and below us, but then it seemed to turn away from us. We couldn't see the mouth of the canyon nor the stream in the far distance because of the turn. As we continued, I kept focused on the bend. For some reason I kept thinking that I was seeing something through the thick trees, but every time I stopped and really focused nothing was visible. It was at one of those moments that Rebekah grabbed my elbow. Right below us was a log cabin. We had passed it by because the trees had it so sheltered.

The cabin looked bigger than ours, but had the same feel and appeared to be in about the same condition. There was no pile of fresh split firewood on the porch, and no hint of smoke from the chimney. It appeared to be vacant, but we continued to study it intensely for several minutes. The window facing us was boarded up. Halfway between the bend in the canyon and the cabin, it looked like we could pick our way down a rockslide. It wouldn't be an easy climb back out, but getting down appeared feasible.

We kept our eyes peeled for movement, but we continued to see nothing. Below us the stream was running through a meadow. We couldn't see the trail, but it had to be there tucked into the deep vegetation. We found it easier to turn around and sit down on the gravel slide and just let it carry us down to the canyon floor. A log helped us cross the stream, which was indeed wider than ours, but still not very deep. The trail was hidden in the tall grass as we suspected, but there were no fresh footprints on the well-beaten path. We headed upstream to the cabin slowly, with our eyes focused on the cabin door.

The door wasn't locked, and the cabin was physically larger than ours, with a loft and two small rooms. It wasn't anywhere near as nasty as ours had been, but it was also clear that no one was living there. There were a couple of pictures of long legged girls from a 1947 calendar that I pretended to be interested in just to spark a rise from Rebekah, but other than that the rooms were empty. There were no rocking chairs and the bed frame didn't have a mattress, but there was a bench on the front porch. We needed to make some decisions. It had taken us over an hour to work our way down from the top shelf to the cabin.

If we started walking down the canyon and out on the prairie grass, it was going to take us the rest of the afternoon and on into the evening to get "home," but neither of us wanted to start back now. What had we come for? We hadn't discovered anything that could help us. However, if we spent much time exploring this canyon, we would be walking back in the dark.

We were prepared to spend the night if needed, and without saying so, that's what we decided.

We both wanted to explore upstream and compare the falls with our personal paradise. We could hear its roar above us; however, we had yet to catch a glimpse of it. I couldn't shake the need to explore the mouth of the canyon first. The well-traveled trail to the cabin intrigued me. It also made me extremely cautious. The thought of splitting up wasn't an option, so we decided to check out the mouth of the canyon. We agreed that we could explore the falls later in the evening, if we had time, or possibly in the morning.

I left the saddlebags inside the cabin door, and Rebekah left her serape blanket folded on top of the bed frame. The trail took us back to where we descended from above and then twisted into the thicker trees. At the bend there was barely room for the stream and trail to pass through the cliff faces. We soon realized that there was another bend in front of us. We were upsetting a large number of birds in the trees as we walked through their roosting areas. That gave me some comfort that no one was immediately in front of us.

When we rounded the last bend, we both dropped to our knees. Less than fifty yards in front of us, there was a large silver metal building lined with multiple windows. Again there was no sign of life. I suggested that Rebekah should stay hidden in the trees, and allow me to sneak up and peer into one of those windows. She could watch me, and perhaps even warn me if danger approached. She agreed.

The windows were without curtains, but there were no windows on the back of the building, only the sides. I moved to my right so my approach would line up with the windowless back. At the back door, I noticed considerable mud leftover from the rain, but no tracks. I gently checked the door, but it was locked. After glancing back to Rebekah, I eased around the side and slowly rose up to peer into the first window. There wasn't much to see. It appeared to be a big room full of beds, army green, steel bunk beds.

Being less cautious, I continued past the windows towards the front door. There still were no signs of occupants. Peering around the front, I saw a concrete slab covered with a metal awning. The metal building wasn't new by any means, but compared to the cabins it was modern. The front door was unlocked and I eased my way inside. It was unoccupied. The front of the building had two side rooms. One was a bathroom with multiple stalls and showers. The other appeared to be an office. The office door was locked, but the interior window showed that I was correct. A desk and old computer were all I could really see.

I walked through the beds and opened the back door waving at Rebekah. She immediately started towards me with some relief on her face. After personally confirming all that I had pointed out to her, I felt the need to check further out front. A short hill blocked my view into the Pampas. I needed to see what it hid. About a hundred yards out, I found the tracks of a truck. It appeared to have driven away in yesterday's rain. The tracks looked fresh, but they had certainly been made before the major rain. In another fifty yards

I could see the gate and the beginning of the road that, like ours, disappeared over the horizon. From here we were probably still a hundred and sixty miles from the main road. We hadn't made much progress.

We decided that we would spend the night in the larger building. The cabin's bed didn't have a mattress, but we weren't sure how we would stay warm in the metal building. We had the one blanket Rebekah had been using, but other than that we didn't have anything but what we were wearing. I stacked four of the mattresses from the bunks two by two, and then stacked two more for us to slide under. It wasn't exactly the best, but it seemed to work, as we lay there tucked away between the mattresses.

She broke the silence in the dark, "I think I know what they use these bunk beds for."

I responded, "I was thinking the same thing. It's a place for persons to be held over. I suspect that the truck we rode in is a transport."

"I can't believe Gary was in this kind of business. It makes me sad to think that he could be involved in buying and selling people," she said with sadness.

We lay there under our mattress for a while listening to the metal building contract as the cold air moved in. Neither of us slept much.

CHAPTER 17

Blisters

The morning couldn't have arrived any too soon. Our makeshift bed had not been very comfortable, but we survived. For the first time Rebekah was up before I was. The water wasn't turned on, so after a quick wash in the stream, we started our trek back to our personal Garden.

We both drank as much as we could, and I took one of the plastic grocery sacks that I had brought. I filled it, and then carefully packed it like a bladder into one of the saddlebags. We almost decided to attempt to climb back out of the canyon and return the way we came. We would have water on that route, but with the saddlebag of water we decided to continue with our plans to stay down low.

After a few hours we were both glad that we weren't attempting to walk out to the main road. If it really were a hundred and sixty miles, then we would need to be planning for at least a ten-day walk. Water would be a major issue. Somewhere about the halfway point, I noticed that Rebekah started walking with a slight limp. When I asked, she said she was fine, but in another hour it was evident that it was getting worse. I suggested that we take a breather.

Without asking, I knelt before her and began to unlace her left boot. She protested but I insisted. The blister nearly covered her heal and was starting to fill with blood. It wasn't a pleasant sight, but it was easy to drain and wash, at least from my perspective. When I replaced the sock and boot, she said that it felt significantly better. She may have been lying, but she could at least walk.

In another three hours we could see our canyon entrance. It was as we had left it; no tracks but ours, nothing was disturbed or out of place. It was good to be "home." We both did our best to resist waving at our "peeping toms" as we passed by.

With Rebekah's feet soaking in warm water, I opened a can of "ham." We had already eaten the canned meats that we recognized, but we had avoided the sardines, mackerel, potted meat and canned ham. Other than another can of salmon that was all that was left. Chopped up with navy beans and served over egg noodles, we both ate quickly and pretended to enjoy.

"Your foot is thankful that we don't have another hundred and fifty miles," I said as I sat beside her after cleaning up the cooking.

"I'm thankful, too," she said.

"How's the foot feeling?" I asked.

She responded, "Better, thanks. I'm sorry."

"Sorry? Sorry for what?"

She said, "I messed up our plans. What are our options now?"

Trying to be optimistic I offered, "Sardines for breakfast instead of ham?"

"You know what I'm asking," she said with dead seriousness.

"Yes, but I don't know what to say. I don't know what to do. I don't know what we should do," I whispered.

With the familiar warmth of our fire on our feet and our hands locked together, we relaxed, slowly rocking our chairs in unison over the wooden planks.

After watching the flames for a season, Rebekah said, "Richard Dempsey, I love you. When you took off my boot this afternoon and treated my blister, I sat there and realized that I love you more than I have loved any man. I wish that we were somewhere else."

"Somewhere other than our own private Garden of Eden?" I said in jest.

"You think that Adam and Eve ate potted meat and beans?" she countered.

"No, they seemed to be partial to apples," I mused.

She giggled and squeezed my hand.

We were greeted the next morning with a significant snowfall. At least six inches had gathered on the steps of the porch. I started to brush the snow off our steps, but I decided that there was no reason. We weren't going anywhere. We didn't need anything, so I just left the snow to continue to stack up on the step, but I did clear a path to the outhouse. After stoking the fire, I decided that we needed a treat. After an evaluation of our supplies, I decided that sweet rolls were in order. We didn't have yeast, but I could make a baking powder biscuit layered with sugar and cinnamon. As I mixed sugar with some canned milk for the icing, the smell of the baking sweet biscuits filled the cabin.

Rebekah sat up in bed as if a powerful imaginary force had pulled her to her feet. She watched as the browned cinnamon rolls emerged, and clapped as I poured the sweet milk mixture over the hot bread. With a hot cup of tea and sticky fingers, our spirits lifted as the gentle snow continued to fall. What our next step should be we didn't know, but at least for a few hours we didn't concern ourselves. We sat watching the hot embers glow as they warmed our feet and hearts.

The next morning the sky was blue as blue can be. The reflection off of the foot of new fallen snow was blinding to our eyes. After refreshing the inside firewood stack from the porch, I snuggled up to the stove. It was time to start seriously considering our options. I grabbed the novel and pencil. It was list-making time. Until that moment I had not considered the idea of literally spending the whole winter here in our cabin. We had what we needed, assuming the food shipments would continue, but mentally we weren't really prepared. The catch to all of our preparations was simple: what happened if we did survive the winter?

As I adjusted myself in the rocking chair, I confessed to myself that I didn't have any expectations that someday our captives would pull up in the truck, congratulate us for our perseverance and haul us to the airport. That's not the kind of people with which we were dealing. They either get the information they want and kill us, or they don't get the information and they kill us. Either way, there was one common denominator. If we were going to get out of this, we were going to have to force a door open somewhere, somehow.

I looked down at the novel I was using to take notes. The blank page was still blank. Until that point, we had been busy. The activities of survival had kept our minds active, but the heavy snow was curtailing outdoor interests. Sitting by the fire, with Rebekah sleeping soundly, I felt for the first time true fear. Until that moment, fear had been more like a sticker in my sock. With a sticker, one stops, extracts it and then presses on. This time fear struck much deeper. It was no longer just a minor irritation. I was afraid, truly afraid.

If I had been alone, it would have been different. In some ways it would have been much harder, but in other ways it would have been easier. The thought of facing solitude would have been terrifying, but the realization that I could see no way to protect Rebekah from the inevitable shook me to my very bones. I wanted to pray. I really did. I wanted to believe, but my faith seemed to have drained out of my heart like our leaky bucket. I truly felt the Lord's presence the other night on the porch after our first snowfall, and then again at our "church" on the log, but now that all seemed like a dream.

Not too long before I decided to retire, I had met with a friend of mine. His wife had been involved in an affair at her business, and he had discovered the "surprise" through reading her texts and e-mails. He was devastated and had every right to be so. A day or so later I met with his wife. She was repentant in every way and deeply disappointed with herself. She couldn't believe that she had let things go as far as she did. She assumed that she had destroyed her marriage. Several times my friend said to me that he still loved his wife, but how could he ever trust her again? As I sat and listened to his grief and anger, I reminded myself that forgiveness was a choice, but trust had to be earned.

After adding a few splits of firewood to the stove, I prayed, "Lord, I believe in you, and I love you, but right now I'm not sure I trust you. You're going to have to earn my trust again. Amen." It wasn't a textbook prayer, but it was honest, and voicing those sentiments brought a new sense of peace into my spirit.

A gust of wind blew and backed up the exhaust on the stove as I sat before its glow. Smoke oozed out, but then just as quickly sucked back up into the exhaust ducking. In a way, I could feel the fear that had blackened my heart suck up and away as well. I didn't fully realize it at the time, and I certainly didn't connect the vacating of fear with the prayer I had prayed, but the fear left, nonetheless.

Rebekah was stirring and softly said, "What's for breakfast?"

Without moving I said, "Vienna sausages with rice, or without rice?"

She laughed and said, "Is the water hot? I think that I would prefer a cup of tea. How deep is the snow?"

"It's almost knee deep, but I cleared a path to the outhouse."

"You are such a thoughtful gentleman," as she slipped on her boots and opened the back door. I could hear her scream all the way till the half moon door slammed.

By midafternoon a warm east wind was blowing up our canyon, bringing milder conditions. The snow started melting, but it would take several days. The trees in our canyon had definitely started to show their fall colors. Some kind of smaller bush that I couldn't identify had turned a brilliant bright red almost overnight. We didn't need it, but we went out and split some more firewood. Rebekah even wanted to swing the ax some, and discovered the joy of watching wood split. It was great to be outside, but it was even greater to be together.

However, in the back of both of our minds was the thought that we had already had two snows. The next one might be here for good. Winter was going to be harsh in the southern Andes. When the real snows and bitter winds set in, it was going to be difficult. We already were suffering from cabin fever, and it wasn't even winter yet.

After replacing the wood that we had used and scrounging up some lunch, we decided to play a game of checkers. The table was extremely scratched up, so it wasn't hard to add a few more scratches to make a checkerboard. Dried limas and kidney beans made good checkers, however it wouldn't be easy to declare a "king." I let her win a few games, but mostly she fell into my traps, to her mock frustration.

Late in the afternoon I decided to go explore our waterfalls. The teakettle was full of hot water, and Rebekah was planning on a private sponge bath. We both needed to wash some clothes, but with the snow we hadn't thought about how to accomplish that task. I did notice that the camera mounted in the tree over-looking our swimming hole was still buried in snow. No one was watching through that eye, but perhaps there were other cameras we hadn't discovered. I wanted to climb the rock ladder and look around up top, but the mist of the falls had covered the wall and sealed it with a layer of ice. It didn't look climbable.

Our fish were nowhere to be found, either. I watched the normal areas where they would hide, but they were gone. A few birds were fluttering around, taking advantage of the warm sun, but generally it was absolutely still. Even the waterfall seemed quieter. The thought of attempting to survive all winter chilled my bones, but as I studied the cliffs, I couldn't think of any other possible solution. I knew that we needed to explore to the north, but what did we reasonably expect to find? Frustration was all over me.

Assuming the teakettle bath would have been fin-ished by now, I picked my way back through the snow. I knocked, and heard Rebekah invite me in. She had the teakettle warm again, and had her shampoo in hand.

Batting her eyes, she asked, "Would you wash my hair?"

She tilted back her head and I poured the warm water over her head into the bucket. Then I scrubbed her hair and head as she relaxed. I poured the rest of the water to rinse out the suds. From the look on her face, it was a marvelous experience.

As she wrapped a towel around her hair, we both heard footsteps on the front porch. We froze. Our minds were racing. A knock came on the door. There aren't any places to hide in a one-room cabin, so together we walked over and opened the door.

CHAPTER 18

Gaucho Gil

It was the "visitor." We hadn't seen that cruel smile since we left Regina in the kitchen. We still had no idea, nor did we care, what his name was.

"*Buenos tardes, my amigos.* I trust that you are warm and well fed," he said.

We stepped backwards as he stepped inside. We caught a glimpse of two other men standing not far away in the snow.

Noticing the towel and obvious hair washing, he said, "My, my, our little cabin seems to be a wonderful honeymoon suite. I may need to remember that. It appears that you two are doing quite well. I'm so very glad you two are healthy."

We didn't know what to say, so we just stood there looking bewildered.

"Did you really think we were planning to leave you here all winter? I hate to disappoint you, and interrupt your little love shack experience, but I need to ask you to get dressed and pack your things. We have a trip to

164

make. A major winter storm is heading this way. If we don't leave now, we might have to spend the winter here together," he said with that cruel smile.

Again, we stood there motionless.

"Now, *pronto*," he barked.

Like robots we started packing our things and putting on our traveling clothes. Rebekah slipped the blanket over her coat as she had been doing most of the time since our hike up top. Once we laced our boots, the visitor invited us out the front door. He didn't offer to help carry our bags. I noticed that he left the door standing open as we started walking towards the mouth of the canyon. I wanted to dart back and close it, but I resisted. What did it matter whether "our" cabin lost its heat? It was now no longer "our" cabin.

At the front gate was the familiar Mercedes panel truck. We were invited into the back as before, but as the rolling door opened we were surprised. We weren't alone. A young man with his hands tied behind him was seated about midway into the truck on the floor. As we watched, he was ordered to step out. They helped him to the ground since his hands were tied.

We were invited to climb in. They tossed our bags in behind us. The young man, with his hands tied, was marched out into the snow-covered grass about fifty yards. In mid-step the man behind him pulled a revolver and shot him in the back of the head. The single *pop* echoed off the cliffs. The lifeless body fell into the deep grass and snow.

Before closing the rolling door, our cruel-smiling guide said, "The Pampas hides many things. Have a safe trip."

The door rolled closed, and darkness surrounded us as we heard it lock.

"He wanted us to see that," Rebekah whispered.

"Yes, I'm afraid he did."

The truck engine started, and our trip began to wherever it was to take us.

The interior of the truck was identical to what it had been. Once our eyes adjusted, however, in the front were several dozen plastic chairs, the kind of chairs one would see anywhere around the world. A bungee cord was holding them attached to the wall, but I eased it from its hook and removed two of the chairs. Not being attached to the floor left the chairs extremely unstable, but it was preferable to lying on the floor.

We recognized the feel of the gate leaving the ranch and then the turn onto the main road. That leg took us almost three hours. It probably was at least hundred and sixty miles. We would never have made it on foot. An hour later the truck stopped and we were invited to use the facilities. It had stopped at a gas station, grocery store and tourist trap combined. Assorted pottery products were scattered over at least a half-acre.

We were allowed to browse the various racks of trinkets and cheap souvenirs. We were watched, but not curtailed. I bought a couple of "Nutty Buddy" ice cream bars and two Cokes with nodding approval from Rebekah. Across the road was a strange memorial of some kind. There were several small shrines and numerous flat rocks with dried up food items. Red scarves and flags were flying all around the memorial. I asked the woman who took my pesos what the shrine was, but she looked at me as if I was a green Martian. All she said was "Gaucho Gil," and quickly turned away.

On a postcard beside the front door I saw the shrine pictured. The back of the card said in both Spanish and English that it was a shrine honoring "Gaucho Gil," who was the patron saint of the poor in Argentina. He was a gaucho, or cowboy, a Robin Hood, a general hero to the poor, and, apparently, a healer and miracle worker. I put the postcard back on the rack, but I thought to myself that we could use the Gaucho about now.

Eventually we were ushered back to our transportation. When we climbed in, we were surprised to discover that we were no longer the only travelers. Six faces were peering at us from the inside of the truck. We had not seen any other vehicle or person while we were stopped, but we had new friends nevertheless. We spoke greetings, but they acted as if they did not understand. Once the door closed and we resumed our journey, Rebekah tried to converse with our new travelers. She spoke her broken Spanish, but she received no response. They were whispering among themselves, at least several of them were.

Two seemed to be sisters, maybe fourteen or fifteen years old. They were wearing new jeans and colorful blouses, but their hair and feet gave the impression that they would have been more comfortable in jungle attire. Two of the others were young men, perhaps eighteen or so. They, too, were wearing new jeans, but they were wearing very traditional walnut stained ponchos with fine red and white stripes. The other two seemed to be brother and sister. The eldest couldn't be much over eleven or twelve. All six of our new friends had very handsome features, but were clearly indigenous to jungle regions.

It also was clear that the three couples did not know each other, and we wondered if they could even understand each other. Their language had a few Spanish words, but generally it sounded uniquely different. We did notice that they all seemed to be very excited, and appeared to be on this trip by personal choice. They obviously didn't understand the nature of the business that was being operated by the associates. That observation puzzled me. I had assumed that slavers would have had to kidnap their victims and force them onto a truck such as this. I would have also assumed that they would have been drugged for control. Perhaps I was staring square into the face of modern slavery.

Our next stop was a quick one. It was already dark outside, but four additional travelers joined us. Very little was said at the stop. Through the night, we stopped another five or six times. At each stop we added from two to six additional travelers. They all seemed to fit essentially the same profile. We eventually unshackled the other plastic chairs and lined the interior walls. Once our fellow travelers understood the plan, they all decided to join us in the chairs, and seemed to be more comfortable and happy.

There were twenty-three of us now, and the smells from the enclosed truck were becoming rank, but Rebekah and I were the only two who seemed to notice or care.

Early in the morning we could feel the truck slow, then turn, and then continue to drive much slower over a different surface. When it eventually stopped, we were all invited to dismount and stretch our legs. There were two blue plastic port-a-potties lined up for our use. After waiting my turn, I walked around to the other side of the truck. Even in the pale morning light I knew immediately where we were. We were at Regina's, or I suppose I should say, we were at Rebekah's new place, but there was no house. In its place was a square pattern of ash. The few items that were still standing in the ash were barely identifiable. The house had completely burned.

The old barn was still there, and between the barn and the house location was a Caterpillar backhoe. Large holes had been dug all around the house area, and even within the burned out house outline. Somebody was looking for something. Off to the side I could see the small safe that had been mounted in the office closet. It had been cracked open like a walnut, probably by the backhoe.

As we were invited to load back up into the truck, I noticed an older woman being escorted to the truck to join us. Her face was covered, but she carried herself with grace. We both knew instantly that it was Regina. Wherever we were going, it appeared that she was joining us. We made sure that she had a seat next to us as the truck pulled away from the river canyon.

Once we were rolling, Rebekah leaned over and spoke in Regina's ear. Rebekah's voice was the last sound she expected to hear, and she immediately pulled away her scarf. Her face had recovered from the earlier event, but now it simply reflected terror. During the week that we were in our box canyon, it seemed clear that Regina hadn't fared as well as we had. Seeing us brought some life back to her face. It certainly did so for ours, as well. She asked if we knew our destination, but we shook our heads. We didn't have a clue.

"My guess is that we are headed to the coast. I'm assuming that we are about to go to sea, but I don't rightly know," Regina said very quietly.

I asked, "Why do you think that?"

"After they took you away, I have been the host to several of Gary's associates. They talked, and most of them didn't care what I overheard. These are bad men. They are *esclavizadores*—they are slavers. They load persons onto a ship and sell them, but I don't know where," she answered.

A couple of the nearest fellow riders looked up when they heard Regina use that term for slavers, but it didn't seem to alarm them.

Regina said, "They think that Señor Black had hidden something of theirs either in the house or maybe buried around the house. They ripped out every wall and have been digging up the ground. I don't think they have found anything. I don't think Señor Black hid anything, either. What could it be that they think he has hidden?"

Neither of us answered, but it seemed obvious that the "associates" did consider $30 million dollars to be of significance, contrary to what the "visitor" had intimated earlier. I didn't know what to say. Rebekah seemed to be terrified. If they really think she might know where the money was, there would be no limit to what they might do to force her to talk.

Since we had watched them kill a man yesterday afternoon, we both felt a sense of darkness over our spirits. There was no hesitation in how the killing had been done. The killer pulled the trigger as if he had been flicking a fly. These people didn't respect life in any shape or form. The more we drove, the more desperate I felt. Desperation can feel like a pack weighted down with lead, and with every mile the pack became heavier. Hope was disappearing altogether.

There were a couple of more stops that we made, but we were out in the middle of nowhere. Most of our "friends" seemed to be getting significantly more excited. I was looking for any opportunity to make a run. If there was a crack anywhere, I was like a coiled snake ready to strike, but no crack came. I couldn't have left Rebekah anyway.

We had been in the back of that delivery truck for hours and hours, but suddenly I felt our speed begin to slow. In a few minutes, we stopped and the door opened. We all climbed out with our bags. The chairs were tossed out as well, and we were invited to have a seat in a large circle. It was obvious where we were. It was near a beach. Off in the distance we could see the ocean in the pale morning light. The first sounds we heard were the screeches of seagulls. Two of our captors were standing nearby, conversing while they smoked. They weren't watching us very carefully.

My face showed my panic. I wanted to start walking. I was sure that if we got a head start without being noticed, that we could make a dead run once we got to the open sand. Just as I was about to suggest this silly plan, I felt Rebekah's hand on my leg. She was looking at me shaking her head, and whispering, "No, no." Was I really that obvious?

Of course she was right, but if not that, what? My misery didn't last long before it turned into terror. Six armed men were walking towards us from the beach. They pointed to seven of the "tourists" and to me, and then in broken English and Spanish motioned us to follow them. We had no choice. Rebekah rose to join me, but was immediately told to sit back down. As I looked back I could she the panic growing on her face. We didn't even have time to say goodbye.

The walk in the deep sand was much rougher than I had expected. If we had tried to run, we wouldn't have gotten very far. Once we reached the shore, we could see our transportation, a powered rubber raft. Out on the horizon was a huge tanker. It appeared that Regina had been right. We were heading to sea.

It didn't take long for the eight of us to be soaked to the bone as the dinghy powered its way into the oncoming surf. It took some time and a considerable chill before we eventually reached the tanker. Stepping onto a lift, we were hoisted to the main deck. The ship was massive in size, at least three football fields in length, but nasty and smelly. Without any words spoken, we were led down a flight of stairs below deck, and down a long passage way. Midway down the hall, doors were opened and we were ushered into our rooms. They placed me into a room by myself, though the others seemed to be in pairs. I assumed that the reason I was alone was so that Rebekah could join me later.

The room itself was surprising. It was much cleaner than the top deck would suggest and had the basics with sheets and towels. There were even power plugs. My laptop might be useful; perhaps even the cell phone might have a signal. I plugged in the phone immediately, but no, there was no service. I wasn't surprised, but I was disappointed.

Knowing there was nothing to be done, I relaxed. It had taken us nearly a half hour to be brought out to the ship on the dinghy. It would take at least two hours to transfer the rest of the group, assuming two additional trips. Rebekah would be here in an hour, or maybe two, depending upon which shuttle she would be riding. All I could do was wait. At two hours, I heard several doors open and then close again. I thought that I heard my door lock snap, but the door didn't open. I wanted to see her. I needed to see her.

Chapter 19

Sea Legs

I still was expecting to see her walk into my room after three hours, but instead I heard the rumble of the engines turn over. The last group would have arrived by now even if they had suffered some problems. The tanker began to slowly accelerate. They would be bringing Rebekah any moment, but my door never opened. With every throb of the ship's engines, I could feel my own heart brooding with disappointment.

A ship that size is a bundle of bangs and rattles. It didn't really matter because I wasn't sleeping anyway. I knew that it wasn't much past noon, but it felt like midnight. In a room without windows, having been in the back of a truck without windows, I really couldn't begin to tell whether it was nearly noon or nearly midnight.

After several more hours I could hear an irritating squeak of wheels coming down the passageway. My door opened, and a porter handed me a food tray.

The door closed behind him, and I heard the lock. A few minutes later I heard the sound of people coming down the passageway. They were obviously walking past my room. They were laughing and even singing, as if they were on their way to a party. I heard a variety of languages, but not English, yet I could not be sure.

Green beans, mashed potatoes, white bread and some kind of once-frozen breaded meat was the lunch offering. While laughing and cuddling with Rebekah's feet before the stove, I could have eaten anything, but alone in that cell I didn't have an appetite. I tried, but it was amazing how every bite was equally tasteless.

About an hour later I heard the party returning. They probably had been invited to eat with the captain. After they passed by, my door opened. The porter asked for my tray and I handed it to him. He left leaving the door standing open. I stood there watching it for a second wondering what I should do, but before I moved, one of the armed guards stepped in and invited me to come with him. I started to grab my gear still thinking that I would be joining Rebekah, but he shook his head no. I was to leave my gear.

He ushered me up to the top deck, and suggested that I walk the rail around the ship. Apparently this was so that I could get some exercise. I walked and he followed. It did appear to be an oil tanker, but I had no way of knowing whether it was loaded with oil or not, but I estimated that it was about the length of three football fields. I noticed that it was flying a flag that I didn't recognize, but for some reason I was thinking Algeria. The coast of Argentina was nowhere to be seen. A low cast cloud had enveloped us and I couldn't even tell which direction we were sailing. I assumed we were pointed east across the Atlantic, but I really didn't know.

After the walking loop and dose of fresh sea air, I was led back to my ship cabin. While outside I had seen about a dozen crewmembers doing various jobs, but I had seen nothing to indicate that this was a slave vessel.

Each day was essentially the same. I would hear the others pass by, and then shortly I would be served a meal. Once a day I would be taken on top deck for my walk. I never once saw anyone else except the crew and the guards.

The plug in my room did have power, and the first evening I loaded my laptop. There was a wireless signal on board, but it was password protected, but at least I could write and make my lists. Most of the time the wind on top would blow your hair back, but in my hole you couldn't even feel that. One night that wasn't true, however. We were evidently in a powerful storm and my room rocked back and forth. Part of me was glad that I couldn't see outside to know how horrible it was, but another part of me was ready for it to just wash me overboard. I spent much of the night hugging the toilet.

On the eighteenth day, the guard came to take me for my walk before I heard the group return from their lunch. I was about halfway down one side of the ship when I saw them emerge from what I assumed was the ship's mess hall. I immediately recognized a few of those from our truck ride in Argentina, but there were at least another hundred additional unknown faces. I watched carefully as they passed across the deck.

With anticipation, I fully expected to see Rebekah and Regina with them, but they weren't there. The last one to pass by had her face covered and maybe walked like Regina, but there was clearly no Rebekah. My heart sank. The only reason that I didn't break into tears was that I refused to allow the guard to see me cry. Once back into my room I had no reason to hold back.

My imagination had run amuck. Perhaps she wasn't even on this ship. I feared that they were trying to make her tell them something that she didn't know. The thought of how they might attempt such a thing simply made me quiver inside.

That night may have been the hardest night I have ever faced in my life. I was a rolling mixture of anger, grief and hopelessness. Over and over I screamed at God, then I would fall into tears until I couldn't cry anymore. Then I would scream some more.

In between my raging bouts of despair, I had this strange notion that if they were physically torturing Rebekah somewhere, she might be doing better than I was. In a twisted way, I starting thinking that if they were torturing me, then I would feel better about my screams and tears. Being treated well with food and exercise, and not being tortured or abused, filled me with shame that I was acting this way, but I still simply couldn't help myself.

None of my teenage heroes would be crying in a cell like this. Rambo wouldn't have cried; neither would James Bond. Marshall Dillon never screamed, and neither did Bruce Willis in *Die Hard*. As I lay on the cot, I realized a truth. All of those men were fictional characters. They never really existed except in the mind of some writer who wanted such men to exist in his fantasy world.

What about the real heroes in this world? What about those Marines who stormed the beach at Normandy knowing up front that many of them didn't stand a chance even to touch the sand? What about Dietrich Bonheoffer marching towards the gallows a few days before his concentration camp was liberated?

Even my history professor from college came to my memory. He had been the mayor of a small city in Hungary when the Nazis swept through. He printed anti-Nazi propaganda, but was captured. Each day they pulled a tooth from his head, trying to force him to disclose the location of the printing press. He never did.

Real heroes in this world do what is right, and are ready to suffer the consequences. There are no superheroes; there are no men of steel who can only be hurt with kryptonite. Real men cry in their cells without shame, and probably would pray the same kind of prayers I had been praying: ugly, raw and honest. Somewhere in the midst of that inward rant, it dawned on me that I was being tortured. What they were doing to me was beyond having my teeth pulled. Their brand of torture wasn't as bloody, but it was just as deadly if I allowed it to be so.

It's hard to describe, but three things happened as I came to that conclusion. First, courage came over me. Realizing that I was being craftily tortured in my mind, rather than just being neglected, gave me strength. Second, my room grew immediately lighter. My desk lamp had been burning the entire time, but the room had dark spots. Those spots seemed to dissipate. The lamp didn't get any brighter, but somehow the entire room did.

Third, this was the strangest of all. Somebody touched me on the shoulder and whispered in my ear. I had been a preacher and a Christian most of my adult life, but faith was generally a decision I made. I had believed in God because I had wanted to believe, I had chosen to believe and I had needed to believe, but to be honest, my faith had always been a constant choice. I had to regularly choose it.

The touch on the shoulder and the word in my ear took that moment in the snow back at our cabin in the Andes, and elevated my faith to a new level. I no longer had a choice. I was not alone and I knew it. No matter what happened, I knew that I was secure. If they marched me out, and held a gun to my head, I would have died knowing that I wasn't abandoned. If they marched Rebekah out, well, that would be a different story...one step at a time.

I spent the biggest part of the next several days singing to myself and to Him. In our church we had sung mostly modern praise music, but in the stillness of my lonely cell I couldn't remember most of the words of even my favorite worship songs. That irritated me. In my cell, most of the songs that I could remember the words were older hymns that I had learned as a kid.

However, I also sometimes would just sing new songs that I would make up as I was singing. I would just sing my prayers, but as strange as that sounds, it felt like I was singing a song in a difference language. I had read about such things, but it had never happened to me. Perhaps in a steel-walled cell, on a ship to "who knows," was where my spirit needed to be in order to slow down enough to learn to sing.

CHAPTER 20

Proposals

Four days later the ship's engines began to shut down. The throb of the diesels grew softer. Even in my hole I could feel the great vessel slow to a crawl. Shortly thereafter, I heard the sound of doors opening and my friends celebrating. Wherever we were, we apparently had arrived. It took several hours before my door opened and I was led to the top deck. It was still pitch dark. There was hardly any hint of stars, and not a light as far as you could see, except the running lights on the ship itself.

The same lift lowered several of us down to the rubber dinghy, and we started our wet, bouncing ride to the shore. By the time we arrived and waded the last few feet in the pounding waves, the sky seemed to be somewhat lighter. The group was gathered where the sand ceased. I looked around, but I couldn't find Rebekah or Regina. There were considerably more armed guards. It was amazing to me that this group still acted excited. It was almost as if they all believed that we were about to enter Disney World. The sight of armed guards seemed to be interpreted as protection, not containment.

I tried to listen to a couple of the guards talk, but it didn't sound like English, Spanish or French. Their faces appeared to be Arab, or at least Middle Eastern, but that might put us anywhere. Three military-type trucks pulled up to the edge of the sand break. As the "tourists" were being loaded into the back of the trucks, I hung towards the back. We had to walk past a fairly thick line of beach grass and it was still more dark than light. This was my opportunity. If I dropped down and crawled into the grass I could bury myself; they might not have counted, and they might not even know that I hadn't boarded one of the trucks until I was long gone.

I made a snap decision. There were no guards directly behind me and the ones off to the side seemed to be pretending to protect all of us, rather than corralling us. Now was the time. In two steps, I would be beside the thickest stretch of grass. It was still plenty dark. However, just as I was planning to drop and roll, a hand reached from behind and touched my shoulder. I didn't think the few stragglers behind me were that close, but it changed my plans. I continued walking towards the trucks.

When I could turn around and look without being obvious, I counted three young men and one of the young girls. They were at least twenty feet behind me, and none of them made eye contact. None of them seemed likely to have reached out and touched me. My adrenaline was pumping, but I continued in line towards the last truck. With only five us to load, I stepped back and assisted the young girl up the steps into the truck. The three men joined her, passing by me. Still none of them looked at me. Just as I was about to join them, a hand touched me on the shoulder again.

When I turned, one of the guards was standing there and motioned for me to step away. He and I stood there together as the three trucks started their engines and pulled away from us. The guard and I walked down the road the trucks had followed. I sensed what was about to happen. I thought I could even hear him check to be sure that his rifle was loaded.

I had seen how unnecessary persons were treated back on the Pampas. I wondered how many steps we would take before he would pull the trigger. I never looked back. My soul was at rest and a song was in my heart.

As the taillights of the trucks disappeared from view, I noticed headlights in front of us. The trucks were gone, but car lights were coming our direction. I still understood what was going to happen, but perhaps the guard behind me wasn't paid to perform such duties. We continued down the sandy lane until the SUV stopped in front of us. Its headlights blinded both of us, but I could see both doors open and two men exit. Once the passenger stepped away from the headlights, I recognized him. There was no mistake. It was the "visitor."

He spoke with his normal controlled humor. "Welcome, my dear friend. I trust that you had a comfortable cruise over. We're sorry that we had to submit you to less than Five Star accommodations, but surely you were well treated, no?"

I still did not know his name nor did I really care to know. I didn't respond to his question. I had nothing to say. The driver ushered me around to the back door and invited me to have a seat. The back seat was empty. We turned around, and started down the same road the trucks had traveled.

Nothing else was said until we slowed and turned down a paved road. Once we were at highway speed, the visitor turned and offered me a bottle of water. I really was thirsty without realizing it. It tasted wonderful, as if it had just been removed from ice. I wondered if the "tourists" were being treated in a similar manner. When would it dawn on them that they weren't going for the purposes they had been led to believe?

"Thanks for the water," I said.

"You're welcome," he said, appearing very satisfied. His plans, whatever they might be, seemed to be flowing without a hitch.

As I sipped the cold water, I realized that my fear of being shot was truly irrational. If they wanted to just kill me, then the Pampas was plenty big and empty. They wouldn't have shipped and fed me just to shoot me on the beach across the Atlantic.

"Where's Rebekah?" I asked.

"Oh, yes, Rebekah...she was a beautiful woman, don't you think?" he said without turning around.

"Where is she?" I asked again.

"I don't think she really knew where that man of hers hid our money. We gave her ample opportunity to tell us...but now that I've reconsidered it, I don't think she ever knew," he said.

The past tense in his words drove a sword clean through my heart, but I contained myself. She's gone, but why was I still alive? The SUV pulled off onto the shoulder of the highway. The "visitor" turned and faced me.

"Our friend Gary kept our business records, but you already knew that. We know that you like your laptop, so we assume that you know how to use a spreadsheet. Am I right?" he asked.

The line of reasoning caught me completely off guard. I didn't have any idea how to respond except with the truth, "Yes, I know the basics of a spreadsheet."

"Good, good, very good," he chuckled, "Here is our offer. We can find many persons who will do our book-keeping, but if we hire an outsider, then we have to explain to them the nature of our business. We would prefer someone like Gary, who may have had a clue, but at least pretended not to know or care. We know that you already know, so if you would be willing to perform such a task for us, then we could all be very happy. Understand?"

"I'm not a bookkeeper. I'm not an accountant. I even dropped out of accounting class in college. I can't do what you're asking," I said.

"That would be too bad. We have already invested much in you. We think you can do the job. If you don't think you can, or simply don't want to, then we'll have to make other arrangements. Currently we are still several miles from any populated area. There's a small road turning to our right. If you prefer not to help us, we'll take a drive down that road. It's your decision," he said.

"You never answered my question. What happened to Rebekah?" I asked with more force.

"If I told you, would that help you make a decision?" he responded.

"It might. Where is she?" I shot back.

"You fell in love with her, didn't you?" he said.

I didn't answer. The engine was running quietly as we all sat in silence for a few moments.

"It looks to me that without Rebekah, you're worthless to us; but with her, you might be willing to work for us and help us out. Am I right?" he countered. I didn't answer again.

"I'm going to take you to a safe house. It will be much more than you expect. You will be treated like royalty. Start keeping our books, and in a few days, we'll see what we can do about arranging for you to see the woman. Good?" he asked.

"So you are saying she is not dead?" I asked.

He just smiled and signaled to the driver to continue on into town. As we accelerated, he turned back and said, "This I promise you. If you don't perform as we ask, I will make you and Rebekah suffer. There will be no polite trips at night with a single bullet. There will be pain; there will be a 'beyond your imagination' amount of pain. Do you understand me?"

"I understand, but I will not touch a single account, invoice or spreadsheet until I see that Rebekah is safe and with me. Do you understand?" I said with equal force. My courage seemed way out of character.

The visitor simply laughed as we entered into the village. I could not tell what city or even what country we were in. The signs seemed to be mostly Arabic, but there was some English. The homes were generally white adobe with stone. I had to believe we were somewhere in North Africa, but I really had no idea. I couldn't imagine that we sailed around the tip of Africa in twenty-two days, but I couldn't guess where we might be.

Most of the women I saw on the street in the city were dressed in black, and the men were mostly in white muslin. The few children I saw were wearing bright colored T-shirts and shorts like kids anywhere around the world. We entered what appeared to be the city square and turned back to our left. About a mile out of town we stopped to allow a gate to open for us. Inside was a beautiful white-columned house, and all around were well-manicured lawns, flowers and trimmed trees. A large party area could be seen behind the main house, with the edge of a pool visible. High walls surrounded the entire compound, but the complex did strike of royalty.

A servant met us in the circular driveway and secured my bags. I think he thought it would be heavier than it was, but since I left the States I had "lost" a few items. As he carried the bags in, the "visitor" snapped his fingers. The servant brought my bags over and set them on the main dining room table.

The visitor unzipped each pocket and began to unpack everything. He carefully reached in and retrieved the laptop. Then he gently dumped the rest of the clothing and toiletries on the table. He popped out the SIM card from the cell phone and tossed the phone back into the pile on the table. After examining each item carefully, he turned to me and asked where Gary's Beretta was. I stepped up, and unzipped a hidden pocket inside the main pouch. I removed it and handed it to him leaving my passport in the secret compartment. He checked to see whether it was loaded, and then dropped it into his own pocket.

Turning to me, he said, "I suggest that you clean up. You're developing a bit of a smell. Anything you need, just tell the help. You have a cook, a housekeeper and a general maintenance man who cares for the yard, pool and does small repairs. What would you like for dinner? Mona, the chef, is outstanding, and by the way, you might want to order for two." With that, he turned and walked out the back door.

I wandered around the main downstairs as I thought about what he meant about ordering for two. The house was beautiful. The furniture was simple but modern, and very expensive. The multiple rugs were intricate and well-suited for the general atmosphere. Even the artwork looked to be expensive. Through the front window I could see the fellow who had carried my bags upstairs. He was already outside, and was on his knees working on the sprinkler system.

Around the corner I found the kitchen. It too was elaborate and tastefully decorated with copper pots and granite cabinet tops. The house was spectacular, but it told me that the "business" I was being pressed to help was extremely lucrative. The chef didn't respond to my greeting. When she finally turned and saw me, she jumped not knowing that I was present. I greeted her again, but she pointed to her ears. She wanted me to know that she was deaf. She walked over to a shelf near the massive stainless walk-in refrigerator and secured a notebook. She opened it and handed it to me with a sweet smile.

It was the kitchen's menu. One column was in Arabic, but the other column was in what looked to be German. I indicated that I couldn't read either, so she flipped the page again. It showed the same lists except in French and English. Glancing down the list I saw two items of the several dozen that jumped out at me. At the top of the list was "lobster thermidor" and at the bottom was an "American Hamburger with freedom fries."

The lobster would have to wait. I pointed to the bottom and held up two fingers, no, I held up three fingers. She grinned and folded it up. She pointed to a clock and tapped on the 7:00. My little watch showed to be 9:00 in the morning. Her clock said 4:00 in the afternoon. I adjusted mine. The thought of a hamburger and fries made me almost dizzy.

Upstairs I found that the housekeeper had already turned down my bed, laid out clean white towels and a swimsuit. I hadn't even met this woman, but she could read my mind. Jumping into the swimsuit provided, I grabbed a towel. The water was simply amazing. It was salty but perfectly clear, and felt wonderful on my tired body. A thick flow of bougainvillea blooms draped over the back fence. The bright reds and pinks were startling against the white adobe.

As I paddled around on my back feeling the cool water, my mind was in neutral. This place was magnificent, but without Rebekah I was miserable. I was still in prison, but this one was nicer than the cabin—especially if the visitor kept his promise. However, if he didn't, then this very pool is where I would probably die. My blood might mix with the blood red blooms. There was no uncertainty in my heart, or fear.

CHAPTER 21

Under the Lion

Upstairs I took a long hot shower. The whole time I thought about what I was planning to do. Keeping the books for the business seemed like the least of my worries. If Rebekah didn't show up, what should I do? How long should I wait? As I watched the water drain between my feet, I resolved again that I wouldn't do one thing until Rebekah was with me; I wouldn't even eat.

All of my clothes were gone, but the closet had at least a dozen shirts hanging that were my size, along with pants and golf shorts. The pants were too big. Apparently I had lost some weight over the last month, but with a belt I made do. One look in the mirror told me that I needed a haircut and shave. I was getting shaggy. As I started down the stairs, I met Katrina. She was the housekeeper and spoke excellent English. She noticed that I had found the clothes and informed me that all the other clothing was being laundered. I asked her about a haircut, and she responded immediately.

In a few minutes she had seated me on the Saltillo tile floor, draped me with a bright yellow cape, and began to trim my hair with her scissors. She didn't ask how I wanted it cut, but she cut it as she thought it ought to be. It was one of the most wonderful haircuts I had ever had. Then she produced a straight edge razor, and with a hot towel brought in by the chef, she cleaned my face and neck as smooth as a baby's behind.

The entire time I kept my eye on the clock. I was very hungry, but should I eat? I had said to myself that I wasn't going to eat until Rebekah joined me, but something inside of me wasn't convinced she was still alive. The whole discussion with the "visitor" left me confused. If Rebekah was dead, then I was ready to die. I wasn't going to play their game. Katrina toweled down my face at almost straight up 7:00. It was decision time. I wasn't going to eat, but I needed to try to explain that to Mona. Perhaps Katrina could help me communicate.

We walked into the kitchen, and at the table sat the "visitor." He commented how handsome I looked after the haircut and new clothes, and how much he personally enjoyed American hamburgers and freedom fries, especially the way Mona cooked them. The smell of the kitchen was magnificent. I stood there with Katrina without speaking.

He slid towards me a paper accordion file across the kitchen bar saying, "Here is enough to get started. Work your way through it, and figure out how best to organize our records. In a few days I'll come evaluate your work."

"I told you I wasn't lifting a finger until I know that Rebekah is safe," I said with conviction.

"What if she has had an accident?" he said.

"Then I'll never help you," I said with firmness.

He responded, "Then you'll probably have an accident, too."

"So be it," I said, looking him dead in the eye.

"By the way, my name is Victor Luwegia. We've never officially been introduced, but since we are going to work together, we ought to be on a first name basis." He extended his hand. I refused.

"I never said that I would help you," I said with firmness in my voice.

"Yes, you did, with one condition," he said with a smile. With that he punched a number on his cell phone, and smiled again. Almost instantly there was a loud knock from the front door. It was produced from the large knocker mounted on the massive wooden front door frame.

Victor smiled and said, "You might want to go open the door. I think it's for you."

I broke and ran to the door. When I opened it, there she stood. It was clear that Rebekah didn't know what to expect behind that door either. It was also clear that she had been convinced that I was already dead. She looked tired, but when our eyes met it was as if she completely lifted off the ground. She screamed with delight, and we hugged and kissed. It was one of the happiest moments of our lives.

After giving us a few moments, Katrina suggested that we might come to dinner. Rebekah really wanted to shower first, but decided that since the food was waiting, we would eat first. When we entered the kitchen, Victor was nowhere to be seen.

Once we sat down, Mona, our deaf cook, marched out with great fanfare presenting three plates with hamburgers and "freedom fries." Each plate was presented in a gourmet fashion arranged on a green leaf of lettuce. All the "fixings" were on a tray on the table, including Hunt's ketchup. It was a treat, but after we had eaten about half, we couldn't take another bite. The cook promised to keep the two halves and the other burger in case we decided that we were hungry during the night.

Upstairs Rebekah found that her clothes had all been taken as had mine. In the larger of the two closets she found a complete wardrobe.

"Did you know these clothes were in here?" she asked.

"No, I never looked. I never even thought to look," I said.

"I'm going to take a bath," she asserted.

"Why don't you see if there is a swim suit in that closet?" I asked.

"There is. I've already seen it," she responded.

"Instead of a bath, let's go swimming," I offered.

She grinned and left to go change. She emerged wearing a terry cloth covering, and we headed downstairs to the pool. By now it was almost dark, and we both jumped in without using the steps. Rebekah immediately went under and swam the entire length of the pool underwater. I tried to follow, but I ran out of breath. With our elbows hooked over the edge, we leaned into each other and kissed. Truthfully, I had never really appreciated a kiss until that very moment.

"Where are we?" I asked.

"I was going to ask you, because I'm not sure either. I think we're somewhere in Tunisia, but that's just because I overheard that on the plane," she said.

"Tunisia? That's in North Africa next to Libya, right?" I asked.

"I think so, but I'm no geography scholar," she said.

"Straight north is Italy across the Mediterranean, if I remember my maps," I said, "But how did you get here?"

"After you and the group were loaded on the ship, I was taken down the coast to a village. From there I was flown in a private jet to somewhere about an hour from here. They told me awful things," she said.

I responded, "Me, too. I was convinced that they had tortured you to death."

We hung off the side of the pool for several minutes letting the coolness of the water relax our muscles.

"They showed me a video. It looked like you. They were beating you, over and over. They did unspeakable things to you. They forced me to watch a little every day, until one day they marched you out into the desert and shot you. It looked just like you. It was the most brutal thing I've ever seen," she said. Her emotions were still close to the surface.

I said, "I don't know how they took such a video. They never laid a finger on me."

"However, something else happened," she added. She paused as if she wasn't sure how to explain what she needed to say.

"What?" I insisted.

"On one of the videos which they forced me to watch... I saw you seated on the edge of a metal bed in a metal room. You were screaming at the top of your lungs as if you were hurting beyond control. I couldn't see what they had done to you, but your face reflected absolute terror. It was more than I could stand, but they forced me to keep watching."

After regaining her composure, she continued, "Just when I could not watch any more, a figure entered the video screen and touched your shoulder and bent down and whispered in your ear. You stopped screaming, and an expression came over your face of absolute peace. I couldn't tell who he was, and the man sitting beside me forcing me to watch didn't act like he saw anything out of the ordinary."

She paused for a moment as she wiped a tear away.

"From that point on I knew that whatever happened, we were going to be at peace. When I saw you being shot in the head, I cried, but... I already knew that you were more than a hero. I knew that you were a man who would willingly die for your faith, and for me. From that time forth, you became my champion."

After letting her declaration linger for a moment, she continued, "By the way, who was that man who came in and touched you? What did he whisper?"

I didn't answer. Any words I said at that point wouldn't come close to what I was feeling.

"Was he an angel?" she asked.

"I don't know, but you need to know that I wasn't beaten, or physically tortured in any way. The only thing in those videos you were forced to watch that was anywhere close to reality was the touch and the whisper. That was true, and perhaps more true than anything I have ever experienced," I said, trying to force back tears of joy.

"What did he whisper to you?" she asked.

I wanted to tell her, but it was so deeply personal the words didn't come out. She sensed that I couldn't find the right words, and decided not to press the issue.

"Turn your head away. I'm going to get out, and you shouldn't see me in this swimsuit they chose for me," she said with a stern voice. She pointed her finger in my face and said, "I mean it, don't watch."

I nodded in agreement, but I wasn't fully committed. Seeing the leopard skin bikini dart from the pool to the door silhouetted against the interior lights was...how I shall I say this, it was invigorating. What an amazing woman she was!

Still balanced on the edge of the pool, I was in a trance. She saw a video of me screaming, but she saw someone touch and whisper in my ear. This was one of the most mind-blowing stories I had ever heard or experienced. I couldn't do anything but just cry with a joy that went to the core of my being.

By the time I got upstairs, Rebekah had already showered and crawled into the massive brass bed. I quickly showered to remove the salt water, and sat down on the edge of the bed beside her.

"I lied," I said.

"You did?" she said, looking confused.

"Well, it wasn't exactly a lie. I just didn't keep my promise."

She asked, "About what?"

"About not watching you get out of the pool."

She grinned and said, "That's all right, I knew you would look. What did you think about that leopard skin bikini?"

"Let's be honest. Right now, right at this very moment, I have never loved anyone more than I love you. I've never been more attracted to a woman as I am to you," I said with some quiver in my voice.

She reached over and grabbed my hand.

"I would like more than anything in this whole world to slip under those covers and join you, but I'm not going to. The way I see it is like this. The one who made us, the one who is protecting us and the one who is with us right now said that it's best if we don't until we're married. I don't think He said that to spoil our pleasure; I think He said it because He loves us and He knows best how things operate. I'm not crawling under the covers with you, but it's not out of a fear of Him; it's because of my love for Him. To...well, to...if we... well it would be like saying that we know better than our Father does. Does that sound too old fashioned?"

Tears were flowing down her face, but they were tears of love and joy. She whispered, "I have never loved anyone more than I love you. You are my champion, and I know that sounds old fashioned, too."

She lay there, and I sat there for several minutes as we just stared at each other cradling each other's hands. Finally she broke the silence, and said, "May I offer a suggestion?"

I nodded. She was under a sheet and two blankets. She pulled back only the top blanket, and told me to crawl under it. I did so—and then with the firmness of a schoolteacher she told me that I better not try anything, or she would punch me in the nose. She made a fist and pretended to extend a right jab to my muzzle. We both laughed, and then fell right to sleep, the pure sleep of the righteous. I had no bad dreams of drowning, or falling or being chased in the desert sand. In truth, I may have slept more soundly than I have ever slept in my life.

When I awoke, the bed was empty. I heard the shower shut off, and in a few moments she came and sat down beside me.

"This is a step up from our cabin in the Andes, but it's still a prison. What do they expect us to do here?" she asked.

It was then that I realized that she hadn't been told what the proposal was, and I didn't really want to tell her. I was ready to die if they didn't produce Rebekah, but now that she was here and all was good, was I ready to stand against the power of this evil? Part of me was sure that I wouldn't, and couldn't, help this business, but another part of me wasn't sure that I was ready to pay the ultimate price for both of us now that we were together. Suddenly I felt the quandary that Gary must have felt. I remembered the words of regret he had written in his confession.

"We need to discuss that, but let's go eat breakfast," I said.

CHAPTER 22

Options

After a wonderful breakfast of fresh fruit and croissants, and after placing our lunch and dinner orders, we moved outside to the glass-covered, wrought iron table beside the pool.

"I need to explain what Victor has proposed," I said.

"Who's Victor?" she asked.

"Our host. Victor is our 'visitor,'" I explained.

"So you two are on a first name basis now?" she said with a touch of shock.

"Let me try to explain. He wants me to do Gary's job as bookkeeper for the business," I explained.

"Don't joke around. That's not funny," she countered.

"I know there's nothing humorous about it, but that's the proposal," I responded.

"You're not joking...don't tell me that you agreed to such an arrangement?"

"Not really...maybe...at the time they made me think that you were dead. They were toying with me.

I told them to either produce you alive or kill me, but without you, I would never help them. I was ready to push the limit all the way."

"Then I knocked on the door of your private villa," she said with a sigh.

"Yes, you did, and you were one of the most beautiful creatures I had ever seen, and then Victor handed me a stack of papers to get started," I answered.

"You can't help them—you know that. No matter what the cost, you can't do it," she said with considerable firmness.

"I know, but what are our options?"

"For me, there are no options. These people are slavers; they are the filthy slime of the earth. I would rather die than lift one finger to help them in any way," she said with force.

"If I was here alone, the decision would be easier, I think. I would just say no, and let the chips fall, but your presence makes it more complicated," I said.

"How so?" she demanded.

"I'm not sure any more. If I have to choose between keeping a spreadsheet or watching you be tortured or killed, I think I will load the computer every time," I said.

"Don't say that," she demanded again.

"I know what you mean, and part of me agrees, but I'm being honest. When I thought they were torturing you, I nearly lost my mind. I'd give my life in a heartbeat to protect you, but pushing some papers around...or letting them...I can't make that decision. Don't force me to make that choice," I said with power.

"How can you say that? You'll become one of them. You'll become just like Gary. One compromise will lead to the next. I can't believe that you're even contemplating such a thing," she said, getting angry. "What would Jesus say about this?"

I responded, "I've thought about that. Many times I have prayed and asked, but I'm not sure that I know what Jesus would do. Maybe creating a few spreadsheets is his way of answering my prayers?"

"Don't say that. Don't ever say that. I watched my husband spin out of control. I didn't know what he was involved with at the time, but I knew he was going down. I'm sure he didn't want it to happen, but it did, and in the end he still lost his life and probably his soul. Don't ever think such thoughts," she said. Her face was flushed.

I didn't respond, and because I didn't, she jumped up and walked away without saying another word. The rest of the day she stayed upstairs by herself. She even had lunch brought upstairs. I didn't know what she expected me to do.

Downstairs was the office. It was well equipped with everything except phones and Internet connection. I scattered the contents of Victor's portfolio out on the desk. If I didn't know what their business was, it would be hard to determine from the paperwork, but that was the problem; I did know.

There seemed to be three shipping points for their merchandise, and three delivery points. The abbreviation "BA" had to be Argentina, and my guess is that, "TL" was Thailand, but I didn't really know what "SL" might be. There seemed to be at least two shipments monthly from each point of origin. Most of the shipments consisted of from a hundred to three hundred "crates," as they were referred to. It struck me that the use of the term "crate" was a way to refer to the persons as less than human. When I turned to the next stack of papers I noticed that each "crate" was coded with three symbols. There was either a "B or G"; and then either a 10, 15, 20, or O; and then one of the following codes: A, L, H, X, or SP.

It didn't take long to assume that the "B" or "G" stood for gender; the middle number probably stood for an age category, but the last column wasn't apparent. I did notice that at least half of the shipments were labeled with an "X," and I assumed that wasn't good for them. The third stack concerned me more than any other. These seemed to be the final dispositions. Most of the "X" girls went from ten to fifteen thousand dollars. The "X" boys went from five to ten thousand.

The "A" classification went for about three thousand, depending upon age and gender, but the "L" crates went for about $2,000. A few of the "H" females went for nearly ten thousand, but most of them went closer to five thousand. I discovered several per month marked "SP" of both genders. Some of them were delivered for $50,000 to $75,000 each. I couldn't imagine why the difference in prices, until I noticed on the back of one of the "SP" persons a tag marked "0 Neg." Delivering a certain "blood type" could only mean one thing. They were being sold to harvest organs, but I quickly put the thought out of mind, but I still had to fight back the nausea.

With a calculator, I estimated that if the stack of invoices I was examining was typical, then on any given month the business was grossing over forty million. No wonder they were ready to do whatever to preserve the business. It was fairly easy to deduce that this was a massive industry. From the "recruiters" to the ultimate buyers, there was a bucket load of money passing hands. In the grand scheme of things, Rebekah and I were minor players, whatever we decided. This machine would crush us in an instant, but perhaps they underestimated with whom they were dealing.

On my laptop I typed "Options" at the top of a Word document. I needed a list. My mind was confused. I wrote the following:

Option One:	*Become their bookkeeper for the long haul—an option, but not a temptation.*
Option Two:	*Refuse to participate at all, and suffer the consequences for both of us.*
Option Three:	*Pretend to participate, but secretly foul up their system.*
Option Four:	*Pretend to participate, but find a way to bring their business to its knees and destroy them!*

I saved the file and sealed it with a password, but as I did, I wondered. Were they watching me over my shoulder? Were there cameras and bugs all over this place? If they had cameras in the Andes canyon, we needed to assume that they did here as well.

A cold chill ran down my back. I should have considered that possibility before now. What did Rebekah and I say this morning that might get us into hot water? The more I reflected on our conversation, the more I thought that if they had been listening this morning, they wouldn't have been alarmed. That conclusion calmed my fears, but also made me sad.

Late in the afternoon I climbed the stairs to find Rebekah. She was in the guest room stretched out on the bed. She appeared to be taking a nap. I sat down beside her, but discovered she really wasn't asleep.

She started to say something, but I leaned over and kissed her on the forehead instead. Then as quiet as I possibly could, I whispered, "Trust me." She didn't move. "Let's go swimming," I said with a wink.

She rolled up and within minutes exited her closet wearing another bikini, but covered by a white T-shirt and towel. She started down the stairs without waiting on me.

When I made it to the pool she was busy swimming laps up and back, which she continued as I watched. On the outside corner of the pool was a waterfall pouring through the paws of large lion. The eyes of the concrete beast looked down into the splash as the stream poured forth. It was as if the lion was both guarding the pool and offering the gift of water. The stream tumbling into the pool made enough splash noise to hide most whispers, if we were careful. The bright red bougainvilleas were trimmed neatly to frame the lion statue. I waited under the lion, as she continued to swim with the gaze of the lion looking down at me. She was angry with me, and wanted to continue to communicate that, but I was finding more patience than I once possessed. I just waited. Eventually she slowed and swam over to me.

She started to say something, but I slipped under water before she could speak. When I came up, I was holding my finger on my mouth signaling her to stay quiet. She didn't understand, but she complied.

We both turned and faced away from the house with our elbows touching. The lion's splash was just loud enough, at least I hoped. Without looking her direction, I whispered, "We need to assume that we are being watched and listened to everywhere we are on this compound."

She nodded with a shiver.

"Here are our options. Please just listen to me before making a comment. Please?" I asked.

She nodded again.

I began, "First, we can sell our souls, take care of their books, and burn in hell."

She turned quickly to find me smiling, and then relaxed, realizing that I wasn't really considering such a choice.

I continued, "Second, we can refuse to participate, and pay the price right here and now." She had no response, but a blood red bougainvillea bloom fell onto the pool beside us. She removed it immediately, tossing it towards the rock flowerbed.

"Third, we can pretend to assist their business, but find a way to foul up their books before finding a way to escape." She still didn't respond.

I continued again, "Fourth, we can pretend to assist until we have enough information to cripple their business and crush them forever."

"Do you think that's possible?" she said looking at me but not even attempting to whisper.

"I've looked through their records, and I think there might be a way. It may take some time. The business slides through too many fingers. Somebody will eventually make a mistake," I said.

"What if we get caught?" she asked.

"Then it's the same result as number two, just later," I replied.

"I would love to think that we shut their filthy business down, whatever the cost," she said with relish.

"I wonder if that is what Gary was thinking with the thirty-million?" I said.

With that she pushed away and continued to swim her laps. I tried to keep up with her, but she was a faster swimmer than I. When we both grew tired, we returned to the lion.

"I think I prefer number four, but right is right, and wrong is wrong. Promise me that you'll never confuse our 'pretending' with the real thing. You also need to realize that while we are pretending, ships are shipping and depositing more kids every week," she said. She said it to me, but she was starring into the eyes of the concrete lion.

"I've thought of that, but I don't know how to stop it. If refusing to keep their books would stop their business, I would willingly pay the price. You would, too, but it wouldn't. It wouldn't even slow them down," I said.

"Let's bring these bastards down whatever it takes!" she said with passion.

"Whoa, such language from such a lovely face, but I'm with you," I responded.

She smiled, perhaps somewhat embarrassed.

"You understand that it may take me some time. I'm going to learn as much as I possibly can about how the organization works. The more I learn the better chance of finding the right crack," I said.

"Why you?" she asked.

"What do you mean?" I asked back.

"I can help. I have been running a business for years, or at least I once did. I wonder how they're doing without me, but I understand exports, imports, invoices, and billing...probably more than most preachers I know," she said with a touch of sarcasm.

"That's probably true, and by the way, thanks. This morning when I said those things... I just hadn't had time to think. I was in such a shock; I really thought you were gone and that they were going to dispense with me. When I opened the front door, I simply quit thinking. You brought me back to reality," I said.

"It's good to know that you would die for me. Do you regret ever getting on that plane in D/FW?"

"Never once. As hard as this has been, two things have happened that I wouldn't trade for anything. You are one of them, and you know about the other one," I said.

She just smiled.

I continued, "There's one more detail that I haven't had the opportunity to share with you. After I was unloaded on the ship, I made a decision to drop into the grass and hide while it was still dark enough. It seemed like a plausible escape plan at the time. I don't really know whether it would have worked or not, but just before I was planning to jump down, a hand touched me from behind. When I looked, there was no one there."

"Had you jumped and hid, they would have found you eventually," she said.

"I know that now, but at the time it seemed like the only opportunity I had," I confessed.

"You wouldn't be with me now," she added.

"I know," I admitted.

"You wouldn't be seeing any of the assorted swimsuits they have picked out for me," she said with a wink.

"Also colorful T-shirt cover-ups," I added.

She laughed.

After a few minutes of listening to the lion's splash, she said, "So you were touched on the shoulder on the ship, and then again on the beach?"

I just nodded. I didn't know how else to explain any of it.

"How long do you think it will take to get enough information to sink their ship?" she asked.

"I don't know, but even when we get it, we have to find a way to get out of this hellhole, or at least get the information out," I answered.

"Yes, it's an amazing 'hellhole.' What did you order for us for dinner?"

"Potted meat with sardines, your favorite," I said.

She splashed me and swam away.

After taking a shower and trying on more new clothes, I started a search of the master bedroom. The walls all seemed to be clean; the pictures, even from behind, weren't hiding any tiny cameras or microphones. I checked every nook and cranny, but there was nothing. The lamps, the furniture, and even under the bed showed nothing out of the ordinary. The last place I looked was the main chandelier. It didn't hold a speck of dust, which I thought was amazing and attributed to Katrina. However, just as I was about to conclude that the room was clean and free, I noticed that one of the four screws holding the base to the ceiling fan was slightly larger than the others. After a close examination of it, I realized that it was a microphone.

Rebekah exited her massive closet wearing a stylish bright orange sundress. It accented the richness of her newly tanned skin. I held my arm out and ushered her down the stairs for dinner. There weren't any hamburgers tonight. We had to suffer through the lobster and fresh grilled vegetables. After a leisurely walk outside, we returned to the upstairs bedroom. I kissed her as we looked off the balcony. The stars were out.

"I'm sleeping in the next bedroom tonight," I whispered in her ear.

"That's probably best. I'm sorry I was so upset with you," she responded. I squeezed her tight and found my way to the other bedroom.

CHAPTER 23

Special Handling

The next morning, after a brisk swim and a wonderful breakfast, we entered the office together. I reminded her, through subtle hand signals, that any place in the house was probably bugged. But in the office there was probably a camera, though I didn't know where.

In a few hours we had the files fairly well organized. There were things we didn't fully understand, but we went as far as we could go. Rebekah even discovered a piece of scratch paper that was a code to how the "crates" were categorized. It's what I had already figured, but it confirmed the worst. "A" meant agricultural, "L" mean laborer as in a sweatshop, "H" meant domestic housekeeper, and "X" wasn't specified, but we knew. The "SP" also wasn't defined. Having already discovered that most "SP" crates were blood-typed, I didn't offer my speculation. Rebekah held up a ledger page dated March 25 sent from "BA."

"There's only one 'SP,' and there was only one of you. You're special," she said.

"Me?"

"It probably means 'special handling' or 'special order.' You're certainly 'SP' to me," she said. It left me with a knot in my belly that I was classified an "SP," but I relaxed some when I discovered that no blood type was listed.

"Let's see how far along we are," a voice came from behind us. It was Victor. We both stepped back and allowed him to examine how we had the papers organized.

As he studied them, I sat down and printed out a spreadsheet that summarized everything we had thus far. There were several columns left blank.

When Victor asked about the blanks, I explained to him that we didn't have the paperwork to complete the details, but he asked, "Why do you think there was a shipment of 'crates' on those days?"

I simply told him I was guessing. The pattern showed normally two shipments a month from the three points of origin. Perhaps some of those shipments were detained or failed to arrive, but probably for most of them the paperwork had been misplaced.

He nodded with approval and then said, "You understand our business better than I do. I assume that you have accepted our offer."

"What choice do we have?" I countered.

Victor continued to study the spreadsheet.

"If you'll tell me what sort of information you want and how you want to present it, then that might help us know how to lay the spreadsheet out," I said.

"Just do what you think is best, until I tell you different. You are a very wise man. By the way, Mrs. Black, we are thinking about entering into the antique furniture export/import business. That's your expertise, no?" he asked.

"There's not enough margin for your tastes," she said.

"You're probably right, but my wife found a beautiful old roll top desk from the mid 1800's in a shop on Charles Street in Boston. A lady by the name of Ruth was very helpful. I believe that was last week. It was a beautiful piece in American walnut. It was expensive, but worth it. At least my wife was pleased," he said with a touch of sinister joy. He wanted us to know that his reach was worldwide.

Seemingly satisfied that he communicated his warning, he set on the desk another accordion file full of paperwork. "These might fill in some of those blanks. Have fun, my friends. You let me know if the house staff doesn't treat you well," he said with a smile.

With that he turned and walked back through the kitchen, grabbing a toasted sandwich that Mona must have cooked to order when he came in. I dumped the file out. It too was full of old invoices, statements, and records. There was also some trash, and overall this pile was "dirtier" than the previous. Rebekah stayed completely motionless. She didn't say anything, but the look on her face confirmed that Victor's wife had knowingly visited Rebekah's store. The blood had drained from her face. I suggested that we needed a swim.

After the swim and a wonderful lunch, we began on the new pile. Within an hour we had most of it sorted. Sure enough many of the blanks on the spreadsheet were filled in with these additional contributions. We could now give accurate gross income figures for the business, monthly, quarterly and annually for the last eight years. It reflected that the business had been growing significantly.

However, there were very few expense records, or even salaries. Perhaps such a paper trail would come later, or perhaps that was never to be a part of what I was to manage. As I examined some of the statements, I had an uneasy feeling that some of these had been prepared by Gary's hand. I retrieved the old fishing journal that was in my suitcase and compared the two handwritings. There was no doubt. Some of this was Gary's work.

By mid-afternoon there was nothing else to do, so we filed it all away and cleaned up the office. The file cabinet was full of hanging file folders, but they were all empty. Even the labels in the folder tabs had been removed, except two in the back and they were blank. Both of us being somewhat obsessive, we decided to clean every drawer, removing everything. When we were finished, we moved all the empty hanging folders to the bottom shelf. The active files consisted of only fifteen simple folders.

Rebekah was about to close it up, when I told her to wait a minute. The two files with blank labels looked out of place in a drawer full of files without labels, so I reached down and popped them out. She smiled making some comment about my perfectionism, and closed the drawer.

I started to just toss the blank labels in the trash, but for some reason I decided to examine them closely. They were blank on the outside, but they had been reused. On the inside both of them had handwritten labels-one said, "BA Exports," and the other said, "TH Exports." I held them up to the fishing journal. It was Gary's handwriting again. I showed them to Rebekah.

"What does that mean?"

"I'm not sure," I said.

"Does it mean that Gary lived in this house too?" she continued.

"It means he used those files, but I don't know about the house. Maybe," I said.

Suddenly she said with force, "Stand up." She was standing beside the file, but I was still seated in the desk chair. I didn't move.

"Stand up," she asserted again, "I want to check something."

I still didn't move, but I knew what she was thinking.

She looked at me in confusion, but slowly she read my face. The bottom of office chairs was traditionally a favorite place for Gary to conceal things, but we had to assume that there was a camera or microphone keeping tabs on us. If there was something hidden, it would be best for us to not find it on "stage."

"Let's go for a walk," I suggested. She smiled and helped me to my feet.

Seeing the cloudless sky without the horizons was difficult getting used to. I had this urge to jump and look over, but a 20-foot wall wasn't easy to jump over. We could see more from the balcony, but still not quite see the horizon. We assumed that as long as we talked quietly in our walks around the compound wall that we couldn't be heard, but we still tried to be careful.

"I'm not sure what to think. Did they bring Gary over to wherever we are as they did with us? Did he live here, too?" she started trying to whisper. She was getting better.

"I don't know what to think, but here's what we'll do. I'll work in the office a little bit tonight, and when I quit I'll turn off the lights. That will give me a second to feel around under the chair before walking out," I suggested.

"There's a pen upstairs by the bed that when you squeeze it, the end of it lights up. That might help," she said. We both wondered what we might discover.

After supper and some leisure time around the pool, I went back into the office armed with the penlight. Rebekah said that she would go change into another new swimsuit, and perhaps cause a distraction by the pool. Assuming someone was watching, they might be more focused on one screen over the other. When I heard her slip out the back glass door to the pool area, I cleaned up the stuff I was pretending to be interested in, and turned off the light. In the dark I flipped over the chair and examined it carefully. I couldn't believe what I discovered.

I tiptoed across the great room and bounded up the stairs. In a few seconds I was in my swimsuit and, just for the fun of it, I eased over to the balcony and looked down at the pool. I wanted to see what she considered a distraction. Rebekah was wearing a tiny black bikini while she was doing some full body stretches beside the pool. I felt quite secure that the man assigned to watch our activities would not have noticed a tiny pen light on the bottom of the desk chair. I certainly wouldn't have.

Just as I slid the glass door open, Rebekah took two quick steps and jumped into the swimming pool. Without the pool lights turned on, the water had the look of jet-black ink. I joined her with a big splash. In another moment we were both beside the lion and its eternal stream of water.

"Was there something under the chair?" she whispered.

"There was a business card taped on by two band aids. You'll never guess whose business?" I said quietly.

"I haven't a clue. You would think anybody in this type of business wouldn't have a business card," she said.

"It's your card," I said, "It's just like the card you handed to me back at the airport in Bariloche."

"You have to be kidding me," shaking her head. "Is anything written on it?"

"Yes, but it made no sense at first look. It's a series of numbers, but who knows for what?" I answered.

"How many numbers?" Rebekah asked.

"I didn't count them, but several dozen, maybe more. Do you know what they might mean?" I asked.

"I know that Gary and Garret both were always playing around with secret codes when they were boys. Mostly they did book ciphers," she said.

She explained that usually it was a simple code, almost childish. They would choose a book, any book that they both had copies of, and then the code was simply the page, line, and word; so page twenty-three, line four, and the fifth word, and so on.

"So three numbers told you the word. That sounds easy," I commented.

"It is easy, if you know the book. Without the book, or even the same edition of the book, it's virtually impossible," she said.

"Are there any books in the office?" I asked.

She said, "I don't think so, but in the downstairs bedroom there is a whole wall of books, almost like a library, but I haven't looked through them."

"We'll have to take a look," I suggested.

"I remember back in the cabin the feeling I had when I realized that Gary probably stayed there after you found his journal. I feel a similar feeling; Gary has probably been swimming in this pool. He may have died in this pool," she said with a touch of sadness.

We hung on the edge of the pool for several minutes. The night was beautiful and the water felt marvelous. We still didn't know where in the world we were for sure, but the nights were nearly always clear and peaceful.

"Assuming Gary did leave a code on your business card, why did he? What might it say, and who did he leave it for?" I asked almost rhetorically.

"Why leave a code at all? I think we know what he feared, but why my card? Did he think that I would somehow find it? Did he think that I would be in this house? None of this fits together," she said into the night air. "Do you have any plan yet on how we could bring down these monsters?"

"No, I don't," I confessed, "except maybe one."

She asked, "What's that?"

"It involves you distracting the whole country wearing that black bikini," I said with a grin.

"I don't know what you're talking about," she said as she splashed me and swam away.

After kissing Rebekah and saying good night, I emptied my suitcase out on the bed in the guest room. My clean clothes were neatly folded on the dresser thanks to the house staff, but in my bag there still was my phone, minus its SIM card, and the phone charger.

There was also the Argentinean romance novel that I had used to make some lists back at the cabin. List makers don't abandon their lists if they can keep from it. I thumbed and looked at what I had written and thought about all that had happened. As I was reflecting, I suddenly had an idea. I grabbed the tiny penlight. Tiptoeing down the hall I quietly opened the door to the master bedroom. I slid my stocking feet on the tile towards the bed and sat down.

"Rebekah, are you asleep?" I asked.

"No, I was just lying here alone wishing that you and I were married," she responded.

"That's not what I expected to hear," I said.

"Sorry, but aren't you a preacher? Don't you do weddings?" she said, and we both laughed.

"How's your Spanish? I saw you reading a novel back at the cabin," I whispered.

"About like yours, not very good, but who around here even speaks Spanish?" she asked.

"This book is in Spanish," I said holding it up in the dark.

"That's the one from the cabin...you brought it?" she said looking confused.

"It's the only book that we know Gary had access to at the cabin, at least that he didn't tear out pages to start fires. Maybe it's the key to the code?" I whispered.

"Crawl under the covers and let's find out," she demanded.

Like two little kids pretending to be in a tent, I read the first three numbers and she flipped to page 104, counted down to row 47, and the first word: '*Dorado*.'

"That means 'golden' I think. What are the next three?" she asked with excitement?

I reminded her to keep her voice down.

"267, 5, and 10," I said.

"*Morir*, death, or maybe dying, my Spanish is rusty... Gold dying... What's next?" she asked?

"105-2-7"

"*Hermosa*, handsome, or maybe beautiful, next?"

"121-4-9"

"*Embarazada*, which means pregnant. Let's see, "Golden dying beautiful pregnant." This doesn't seem to be making any sense," she said.

"Let's try one more," I suggested, "83-12-8."

"*Ricardo,*" she whispered, "That's either you, or the love interest in the book. His name appears on every page," she said losing some excitement.

"Shall we try just one more?" I said not wanting to give up or leave from our private little rendezvous.

"Sure," she said.

"104-11-3"

"*Nubes,* clouds."

"This isn't working is it?" I said sadly.

I switched off the light, but remained under the covers cross-legged facing her in the dark. I kissed her on the cheek and whispered, "I better get out of here." I rolled out, slid away in my stocking feet, and closed her door.

The next morning Katrina brought into the office a cardboard box stacked full of "business" papers saying, "Victor asked me to give you this if you seemed to be caught up with your bookkeeping."

When we opened it, the first thing I noticed was the ledger that had been in the safe at Regina's. I remembered seeing the safe crushed like a clam off to the side from the ashes. The box appeared to be papers that had been taken from Gary's desk before we were there, as well as after. Much of the paperwork had to do more with the expenses of the business, but not necessarily the income. Notes were written on napkins, paper sacks, store receipts and candy wrappers. There was even a check left blank, but signed, in the amount of $2,300. It had not been deposited or cashed. Most of the notes were dated, but it wasn't clear what the expenses were designated towards.

This was going to take some time. We started sorting it all out into at least a dozen piles, but there were some things we couldn't decipher their purpose. We made a pile and just labeled it "Unknown," but as I was dropping the "unknowns" back in the box, I noticed a little piece of torn cardboard. It was a bar code, but more precisely it was an ISBN number. It was the International Standard Book Number to a book, but we didn't have the title. In a few minutes on the Internet I could tell the title and author. In another minute I could order a dozen copies and have them shipped anywhere around the world, except to us; I would have had to have an address for that.

Occasionally, I noticed that my laptop's "Wi-Fi" signal would blink. However, when I would try to connect, I found a password-protected signal, but it was never on for long. My guess is that somebody in the house was switching it on and placing a food order or something, and then switching it right off. The cook might have been deaf and dumb, but she probably was also very smart. Whatever else she was, she was a great cook.

Out the back of the kitchen, through a swinging door, was a small hallway with several doors. Our guess is that these were apartments for the cook, housekeeper and maybe even the handy man. There was also probably a washroom, and maybe even a communication room with phone and computer. That stuff had to be somewhere, and that's the only place we didn't feel that we had access. I had an idea that I thought I could at least attempt without harm. Normally, most software needs an update from time to time, but most computers connected to the Internet do this almost automatically. If I explained to Katrina that my computer was slow and needed to update, then maybe I could persuade her to allow me access to the Internet. It was a long shot, but it seemed harmless to try.

With it unplugged, I explained my "problem" to Katrina as she breezed by. At first she seemed confused, but at last she nodded in excitement. This was going to work, but Katrina wasn't tricked. She grabbed my laptop and carried it out the back door of the kitchen ordering us to wait.

In less than five minutes she reentered and said, "No updates were required, but you did have several e-mails that downloaded all at once." She sat it back down before me. Strike one.

I glanced through the e-mails. There were hundreds of them. Several dozen of them were from my daughters; they were worried because they hadn't heard from me. Another dozen or so were from my travel agent, wondering about the trip to Israel I had been trying to schedule. It appears that Iran shot down one of Israel's drone spy planes, and the State Department was warning all tourists to reconsider travel to Israel. Three e-mails were from a young woman who wanted me to perform her wedding in December. Many more were friends who were just checking up on me. The last 100 or so wanted me to think about buying my Cialis or Viagra from them. Most of them were in Arabic. I just laughed.

I felt for my daughters. I wondered what they might do, and how long would they wait before they did it. They weren't going to find me in Argentina, and then I remembered that I didn't even tell them that I was going back to Argentina. I didn't want to have to explain anything. I wasn't ready to mention Rebekah at the time. I wasn't sure what they would have said, but now, not having heard from me in six weeks, I can't imagine what they would be thinking.

CHAPTER 24

The Book and its Cover

The next several days were uneventful. We spent several hours each day trying to piece together the expenses from the scraps, but we didn't get very far. Recruiters, if that is the appropriate term, were paid a little, very little. Occasionally a recruiter would get a big tip for filling a special order, but their regular income wasn't much, especially compared to the amount of income that was being generated within the organization. The network of team members, like Victor and obviously many others, reflected no records of receiving salaries, but surely they all were taken care of, probably very handsomely.

The one consistent expense that seemed to be out of control for the business was transportation. Various tanker ships routinely slowed down off the coast of several places around the world to receive or drop off a shipment. The ships appeared to be receiving a thousand to fifteen hundred per head for safe delivery.

We speculated that such income probably didn't get added into the ship's log.

There was a pattern to how the villa operated. Chef Mona, from what we could tell, never left the compound; we never even saw her outside the house. She was extremely attentive when it came to meal planning, but concerning any other request she relied on her deafness. The housekeeper, Katrina, however, would do whatever we asked to make our stay comfortable. Most considerations were provided before we thought to ask. We did notice that she would walk to the main gate, usually twice a week, and be gone for several hours. We assumed a car was kept outside the walls, or maybe she used a taxi. The handy man was never consistent. When there was something needed, he seemed to be always available, but his yard-keeping schedule had no regular pattern. We never saw him clean the pool, but it was always spotless. We occasionally saw him mowing or trimming shrubs, but he seemed to keep his distance from us.

We never saw any of the three carry a cell phone nor were there telephones in the house. There was an intercom system, but it was never used. We noticed that at least twice a week a delivery truck came to the main gate, but it never entered the villa compound. A modified golf cart would meet the truck outside the gate and haul back multiple boxes of food and household items. There didn't seem to be a car on the compound, even in the garages. The few times Victor showed up, even he did not drive a vehicle into the compound enclosure.

There were also a number of security cameras all around the exterior. Inside we assumed there were cameras, but we never found them. We did spot several microphones, like the one in the bedroom, but we did our best to not discuss our feelings or plans except under the lion fountain.

Victor would show up every two weeks or so. He would always ask if we were being treated well, as if our comfort was his number one priority, but we noticed that Mona and Katrina treated him very well. We were quite sure that their loyalty would be with him if push came to shove.

We had no doubt that if we had tried to sneak into the forbidden hallway beyond the kitchen, or tried to talk them into anything that might help us escape, it would be reported to Victor immediately. My mind was always working, trying to hatch a plan of escape, but week after week it became harder and harder even to imagine. We did finally confirm that we were in Tunisia. A couple of the boxes Katrina brought us for the office had shipping lapels on their bottoms. They both had been shipped from Germany to Al Hammah, Tunisia. We weren't sure how that helped us, because we didn't know where Al Hammah was, but at least it was something.

Our normal routine was a morning swim, a leisurely breakfast, time in the office if there was work to do, or in the library if there wasn't. Christmas came and went without either of us mentioning it.

Most of the books in the library were in Arabic, but there were about a hundred books in English. Most of them were cheap westerns or Nazi thrillers, but we both found a couple of volumes worthy of spending some time reading. After all, we didn't have many alternatives. After lunch we usually would play a game of checkers or chess and just visit. We talked about everything under the sun without any limits, except the one thing we most wanted—a plan to escape and go home.

When either of us had a thought of how we might escape, we waited until our afternoon swim and our private time under the concrete lion. We thought of every possible scenario, but with every plan it was essentially impossible once we thought through the mechanics. We both had grown so comfortable that I was afraid we no longer had the courage to attempt a daring run. In truth, we were pampered show steers waiting for slaughter.

I was certainly getting restless and frustrated, but I didn't know what to say. Rebekah was the one who finally voiced our fears under the lion one afternoon.

"Gary obviously handled their money. He would have been moving it around, laundering it, and investing it. He couldn't have siphoned off thirty million without having his hands on much more than that. We haven't been given that opportunity. We just shuffle papers. Without touching the money, how are we ever going to hurt them?" she said showing her frustration.

I had kept a file of everything that had come across our desk. I had the names, or partial names, of over seventy-five individuals and six ships. Granted it wasn't very complete, but in the right hands we might have had enough to at least slow them down. I didn't know how we could obtain any more information.

The hopelessness began to take a toll on us. We felt guilty. We were aiding a filthy and disgusting business that bought and sold people and then used them like scratch paper. One would think that the market for such "crates" would eventually run dry, but apparently not. The demand seemed to be as strong as ever. We both started having dreams at night, probably more accurately nightmares. We hadn't prayed together since the first week we had been there. We were too busy swimming and eating Mona's delicacies to really pray, but really it was the guilt that was eating us up.

Our plan was to discover a way to crash them on the rocks, but we hadn't even come up with a plan to splash a little water in their faces. We were slaves ourselves, well-treated slaves but slaves nevertheless, and we were assisting our fellow slaves into slavery. The pressure was mounting inside both of us. Some days we avoided each other. We just had nothing to say. In my mind I kept thinking about some of the words Gary wrote in his confession, words that haunted my mind.

I could see him in my imagination alone in the cabin and terrified. He was writing knowing that probably no one would ever find his journal or care about his heart. Phrases like "no way out" and a guilt that had "forever stained his soul" would catch me from behind. I knew how he felt when he wrote, "I am beyond redemption in God's eyes," and "I deserve it and worse." There were some days I just wanted to cry, but I couldn't.

When we first read Gary's confession, I was so self-righteous. I judged him; we judged him. I remember asking what kind of man could do these horrors. Now I knew. He had not been any different from any of us.

I longed for the touch, but it wouldn't come. I honestly wondered some nights if I had "shipwrecked my soul." Paul in Timothy, or maybe Thessalonians, talked about two men who shipwrecked their souls. I couldn't even remember which book it was in. It was like all that I ever knew had been drained from my spirit. When I attempted to pray, all I could muster was, "I'm sorry." I repeated it again, and again. I was ready to throw the files into Victor's face and hope that he would put me out of my misery.

Rebekah was swimming, and I was trying to read a novel about a man who was captured by the Nazis. He agreed to betray his neighbor in exchange for protection. The more I read, the more I identified with him. Real evil can't be played with. It will always consume those who toy with it, whatever their motive for playing. It made me so angry that I threw the paperback book across the room.

Rebekah and I had sorted through the books early in our stay. If it was English, we put it one a separate shelf. We generally avoided all the Arabic titles, but when I went to pick up the book I had thrown, I grabbed a few titles off the Arabic shelf and just thumbed through them. Arabic script is strange, but at the same time it's almost like poetry in the way it flows on a page. It would be a pleasure to be able to write a script like that. I thumbed through several various tomes. I wondered what they said. Were they novels, poems or history? Maybe some were biographies, or discussions about faith. There was one particular set that seemed to be a series. The green leather binding all matched and the books were quite attractive.

A quick scan over several shelves showed at least a dozen volumes in this set all with different titles. I didn't know what they were about, but for some reason I decided they needed to at least be on the shelf together. I set about to accomplish that. After gathering them from their various locations, I cleared a spot for them to go back on the shelf together.

When I slipped the fifth volume into its new place, it felt lighter than the others. When I opened it, my heart skipped. It was an English Bible. The cover had been torn off of the Arabic book, and had been used to wrap and possibly hide the Bible.

At home I had a shelf full of Bibles—at least thirty or more various translations. On my desk during my entire ministry, I had at least three at all times. Two had wide margins for note taking. One of those I used to jot down my own personal thoughts. The other I used to jot down the thoughts of others. The leather one I never wrote in. I only used it to preach, but the last several years of my ministry I quit reading all of them. I still had been using the Bible every day to prepare, but I had all but given up reading the Scriptures to nourish my own spirit.

I was like a man dying of thirst who assumed the water he was seeing was a mirage, only to discover that it was actually a clear and sweet pond. I sat down and read the Gospel of John as if I had never read it before. I wept great tears when Jesus told the woman at the well in Chapter 4 that he could give her living water, and then in Chapter 5, I could only hold my heart when Jesus ask the crippled man if he wanted to be well. I screamed at him to say, "Yes!"

Katrina peeped in to see if I was having a heart attack, but I grinned and waved her on. I had to keep reading. What did the five thousand folks really think about eating such special bread? What did the priests think when Jesus interrupted their temple worship by asking if anyone was thirsty? I almost got up and danced with the blind man when he regained his sight in Chapter 9. I did get up and waltz with Lazarus and Mary in front of the empty tomb. Martha had been too busy to join us.

When I came to Chapter 14, I cringed. I had read the chapter hundreds of times at funerals—this time it was alive and breathing on its own. I could feel its hot breath on the back of my neck. Jesus was speaking those words to me, directly to me, when he said, "I am the way, the truth, and the life."

That's when it dawned on me that there was probably a camera, or at least a microphone in the room, but I really didn't care. By the time I reached Chapter 19, I could literally feel the nails being driving into my own hands and feet. I could sense the great stone being rolled over me as I lay there dead beside Jesus in the tomb.

Then came Chapter 20 with the stone being rolled away, and I was standing with John as he looked into the empty tomb, and like him, I saw and believed. I even helped the disciples haul in the net load of fish that wouldn't fit into the boat, and I sat beside Jesus in the sand at that "first" breakfast. Tears of sheer joy were pouring down my face as I sat in the library clutching the "book" to my chest. I was born all over again.

Rebekah had been standing at the door watching me for at least five minutes, before she said, "That must be some book."

I motioned her to come sit beside me. She did so. I leaned over and whispered, "I don't know what is about to happen, but it's going to be good. Get ready, it's going to be real good." Then I handed her the treasure.

She looked at it very confused and said, "I can't read Arabic."

"I think you might be able to read that Arabic. Open it up," I suggested.

She opened it to Jeremiah and gasped when she saw the page. "It's a..." she started to say, but I shook my head and quietly reminded her that we were probably being watched, or at least listened to.

She nodded in agreement, but when she looked down she saw one verse, big beautiful tears began to roll down her face. It was Jeremiah 15:21. She held it up so that I could read it, too.

> *I will save you from the hands of the wicked*
> *And redeem you from the grasp of the cruel.*

We stood up and just hugged each other. Our tears mingled together as they fell on the expensive Persian rug. We heard the dinner bell as I whispered into her ear that something good was about to happen. We simply had to hang on and stay ready. We walked to the kitchen holding hands.

CHAPTER 25

Open Gates

In the morning sun we awoke as brand new people. We had our morning swim and breakfast, but we laughed together. We understood joy even in the midst of crisis.

Instead of going straight to the office we went up to the upstairs balcony. We read from the "Arabic" Bible and prayed together. The morning appeared to be brighter. The birds around the compound were singing louder.

When we finally went to the office, we discovered another accordion file on the desk. We assumed that Victor had dropped it off during the night. It was the usual collection of invoices, scribbled statements, and bills. As we sorted through the pile, Rebekah found two invoices that were stuck together. She set it aside waiting to deal with it after we had handled all the other various scraps and notes. She didn't want to know what had stuck the two invoices together. I didn't blame her, but finally it was time.

She carefully pulled them apart only to discover a sealed envelope between the invoices addressed to "R and R." She didn't think much of it, until she opened it. Then she realized "R and R" was the two of us, Richard and Rebekah. This was a letter to us. Who knew that we were there? The note was simple and to the point. It was typed and read:

Dear Richard and Rebekah,

I trust that you will find this letter. Next Wednesday, January 8, there will a truck delivering some items for the villa at 7:00 PM. Create a diversion of some sort, perhaps a fire upstairs. That will cause everyone to rush to help. It will be nearly dark; so in the commotion run down the side of the eastern wall to the main gate—the eastern cameras are not in working order. The front gate will be left open. I will be waiting, but we will not have much time. Do not delay, and do not forget to bring your file that can sink ships.

Signed, R

She handed it to me to read, and then suggested that it was time for a swim. We hurried as quickly as we could to change and meet at the lion fountain.

"Who do you think R is?" Rebekah started.

"I have no idea. Do we even know someone named 'R'?"

"My partner that runs the business back in Boston is Ruth, but she doesn't even know where we are."

"My secretary at the Church was Robbie, but this can't be her."

"The two brothers from Texas that fished with us were Ben and Robert, but no way could it be Robert," she continued.

"What about Regina?" I asked.

"That would be amazing. If she had any opportunity, I think she would help us," Rebekah said.

"Who else could it be?"

"I don't know. What do you think we should do?" she said in a hushed tone.

"Do we have a choice?"

"Yesterday afternoon you whispered in my ear that you believed that something good was about to happen after you found that Bible. Is this it?"

"I really don't know, but I think we need to be ready to have a little fire and smoke on Wednesday."

"So you think this is legit?"

I thought for a moment before saying, "I think that sometimes we simply need to trust. This may be one of those times."

"What if it's a trap?"

"A trap?"

She continued, "Yes, what if Victor wrote this as a test, a test to see if we would be loyal; to see if we have been preparing a 'damning file,' a file to 'sink ships?' What if he wants to start trusting us with actual money? What if—"

I put my finger to her lips and said, "Sometimes you just have to trust."

"If it really is Regina, what a story she will have to share." I nodded in agreement.

The day we received the letter was Sunday. On Monday Victor came by, but he didn't have much for us. He wasn't his normal confident self, but he didn't seem to be upset with us. He was clearly worried, but he hardly spoke to Rebekah and me. He grabbed a sandwich and mumbled something about the fickleness of people, and then he was gone. It seemed odd for a slave trader to be worried about people.

We followed our usual routine, but I made a couple of copies of our files on CDs. A few weeks before, I had knocked some papers behind the desk. In retrieving the mess, I discovered a small zip drive, so I loaded what we had on it as well. At the time I didn't think much about it. We decided at our private pool meeting spot to pack the minimum. We would take just one bag with a couple of sets of clothes and my laptop. The rest we would leave. The thought of having to run very far made the decision easy. Without really discussing it or coming to a joint decision, we both knew we were taking the opportunity.

A fire seemed simple to plan, but how were we to set it? How long would it take before it triggered the alarm? How would we evacuate? Who would discover the fire? What if we were seen trying to escape, or what if we were stopped? By Tuesday we had our plan. The bag would be packed and left in the downstairs office. All we would need to add would be the laptop. We would spend the day as usual and be ready for dinner at the normal 7:00 hour.

The last thing we would do before coming downstairs would be to light a candle. We "borrowed" a candle from a decorative lamp near the top of the stairs. We found a box of matches in the bottom drawer next to the pool house toilet. I cut a slit in the sheer curtain and inserted the candle tightly. It hung in there at a 45-degree angle. When lit it would take about five minutes to melt the wax to the point where the flame would be shooting up against the curtain. We believed it would work, but we didn't have any way to really test it.

Tuesday night during our swim, we prayed at the great lion fountain. We had a peace about the attempt, but we didn't understand much else. All day Wednesday we tried to relax, but were generally unsuccessful. We tried to read, but didn't flip many pages. We went into the pool twice, but the water seemed heavy and thick. The day lasted forever; the second hand seemed to be crawling around the dial.

At 6:00 we showered and dressed. With five minutes till supper, I lit the candle. At exactly 7:00 we were seated at the dinner table with our boots laced up tightly. At 7:04 we heard the fire alarm squeal. Katrina came bolting from the hallway behind the kitchen screaming. We just sat there like we didn't know what to do. The yard keeper came bursting through the front door and bounded up the stairs. Mona just continued preparing to serve dinner unaware of the deafening squeal. In the commotion Rebekah and I slipped to the office for the bag and laptop, then across the great room, and out the open front door.

In an instant we were running full speed along the eastern fence in almost total darkness. We knew the path because we had walked it almost every day. In less than a minute we arrived at the main gate.

Two men attired in military dress charged into the compound and started running towards the house, apparently responding to the fire alarm. Even in the darkness we could see that there was already considerable smoke in the air. Those drapes must have been quite flammable.

We swallowed hard and slipped through the gate, bolting across the small parking area. No one seemed to have seen us. No sooner had we crossed, than a white Mercedes sedan pulled up next to where we had hidden. The back door opened. The driver stepped out and just stood looking around. With the sedan's interior light we could see that it was Regina. We were hiding not 20 feet away. We came out, gave her a hug, and climbed into the back seat. We were off and we were free.

Regina didn't speed, but she didn't slow for any reason either. Within five minutes we were on the highway heading towards the coast. She explained that we needed to meet our contact in exactly one hour.

She told us that she now belonged to an organization that was committed to destroying the terror of human trafficking. She confessed that she had had her suspicions for several years, but Señor Black had always denied it. She continued rattling off her story, "The last time I saw him he told me that my fears were correct, and that I should flee when he gave me the signal. The signal never came.

"When Victor showed up, he told me that Señor Black told him that I should stay at the house until he returned. When I began to question him months later, he told me that it would be very bad for Señor Black if I quit my job at the house. I didn't want to continue, but I didn't want Señor Black to get into trouble either."

She continued, "After Victor slapped me and took you two away in the truck, I called my friend. She came and picked me up and took me to Buenos Aires. I met with an underground group, which is seeking to destroy this plague upon our people.

"They believed that you two had joined the slave organization, but I argued that such was nonsense. I knew you wouldn't have done that. There is an insider in their organization that for the right price will leak certain information. That's how we found out where you were."

"Where are you taking us?" I asked.

Regina explained that her underground organization had a safe house in Sicily. We were going to board a cruiser and be taken across the Mediterranean during the night. She assured us that we would be safe. She also assured us that if we had any information that could help, her organization had the legal connections to get it to the proper authorities.

She explained, "Your information, plus what we have been collecting, may be enough to crash the whole filthy organization." She sounded extremely excited.

We asked her how it had been that she was personally tagged to help spring us?

She explained that she volunteered, and that, after all, no one else could identify you two. She said that she had been thrilled to do so. The hidden letter between the two invoices had been her idea, but our secret contact was the one that had gotten it added into the box. We didn't know what to say. This could have been extremely dangerous for her.

"If you had been caught, it would have been the end. You took a great risk. We couldn't be more grateful," I said with deep gratitude.

We were pulling into a populated area, but there was very little traffic out. It was nearly 10:00 PM, but Regina assured us that we were close. We could see glimpses of a bay through the houses and buildings. Eventually she slowed. She was looking for Dock 22. Almost as she said it, we all saw the sign.

She asked us to wait a moment in the car while she walked down the gangway. We could see a man shake her hand, but then turn away. Regina came back to the car and told us that we were in the right place. She parked the car, and led us back down to Dock 22. All three of us stepped on board a deep sea fishing vessel named the *Verde Mermaid II*, based out of Milazzo, Sicily. We met the captain, and within minutes we were quietly trawling down a canal.

After we made a quick turn from the canal, we were in open sea. Slowly he opened the throttle until we were at full speed. We were barely skipping over the waves. Moonlight was reflecting off the top of the waves in front of us. The sound of freedom was more than pleasing. In the dark I think both Rebekah and I were fighting back tears.

It's hard to describe how we felt. Crossing the Mediterranean to Sicily would take several hours so we were invited to go below and get some sleep. We lay down on the bunk together, but we didn't get any sleep. The yacht was flying towards our freedom.

We were too excited. Eventually Regina came down and joined us. We were both very curious about the organization she had joined. We were thinking that we might be interested in being a part of such an organization, if they were really able to do what they claimed to do.

We discovered from Regina that they were based in New Orleans, and that the Mississippi corridor was one of the most prolific areas for "recruiting." We both raised our eyebrows when she used the term "recruiting." She encouraged us to try to get some sleep, but we were still too wired. It was hard for us to imagine that after almost eleven months we were now free. The emotion of it overcame Rebekah, and she curled up on my shoulder and sobbed. She had earned the privilege.

CHAPTER 26

Decoding Trust

Regina woke us up and said that we had about twenty minutes. She had some *empanadas* and hot tea for us when we emerged from below. As we ate we could see the Sicilian coastline. It was beautiful in its ruggedness. We could see a number of beautiful houses hanging from the top of the white rocked cliffs. We fell in love with Sicily before we ever set foot on shore. As we prepared to disembark, Regina explained the plan. We would be meeting two young men wearing orange jackets. They would be our transportation to the safe house.

We would need to be prepared to stay at least three to four days to see whether the "associates" were seeking to follow and track us. If not, then arrangements would be made to return us to the States. She asked if we both wanted to fly into Boston. We assured her that Boston would be more than acceptable.

Our vessel smoothly deposited us on a landing slip in the bright morning sun. Two 20-year olds in orange jackets graciously assisted Rebekah up the steps and carried our bag. Regina didn't seem to know them, but the two seemed to know all three of us. We walked quickly to a parking area and entered their new black Fiat mini-van. The van maneuvered the narrow, winding streets with ease. The driver certainly seemed to be accustomed to the roads. It was amusing to watch and listen to him scream and shake his fist at the other idiot drivers as they yelled back at him. I was glad that I didn't have to drive. I secretly wondered if after a year, whether I even could drive.

Leaning over the seat, Regina told us that we would be meeting Steve and Reggie. They would want to see the information we had and might want to ask questions if they saw something they didn't understand. They would be looking forward to meeting us and seeing our information.

Regina then said, "The talk around our office is that you two are heroes."

That term made me chuckle a bit as I had a brief flashback to the night on the oil tanker. I think Rebekah understood what I was thinking. The wail of sirens passing us made us instinctively hunker down. We both laughed as we realized that we both had done the same thing. Neither of us had heard a siren since we left the states last year. Going home might throw us into some level of culture shock.

Our driver turned up a quiet street with tall, narrow homes. At the end, in a cul-de-sac, we stopped. Our two orange-jacketed delivery drivers stepped out and cautiously surveyed the area. All appeared to be safe. We walked up the sidewalk and entered a beautiful home. Steve and Reggie were indeed very excited to have us. They brought tea and cookies out for us and loaded one of the CDs that I produced.

At first they didn't understand how this would help, but I stepped up and suggested that they should open the hidden columns. That's where the names of over 75 individuals were listed, and their general locations. It even included the names of the ships that we knew were contributing to the business. They were impressed, and said so. After about an hour of investigating the files, they asked if these files were still on my laptop. They also asked if I had made more copies. I thought that was a strange question, and for some reason I told them no. I really just made two copies to be sure that I would still have one if somehow one had been damaged.

They then started asking us details about our adventure. Who had we met and whom had we seen? We confessed that other than the house staff, the only one we knew well enough to recognize would be Victor. They wanted a detailed description of his looks, but it appeared to me that it was more for them to convince themselves that we had really seen Victor. After going through all that, they produced a photo and asked us if we recognized him. We nodded. It was Victor.

We were then told that we would be taken to another house that would be safer. There we could order some food and watch an NFL playoff game, or maybe a qualifying game for the World Cup. From what we could gather, Argentina was playing Italy. We pretended to care, but truthfully we cared about neither. I asked if there was any possible way for me to contact my daughters. Who knew what they are thinking by now? They were already worried about me before I disappeared. Rebekah also wanted to call her office.

Steve told me that it would be better to wait until we arrived at the next location. He assured me that an untraceable mobile phone would be available for both of us. We would be there in less than an hour. He also asked us what kind of pizza we preferred. We both answered in unison, "Vegetable." The five of us loaded back in the van and started leg number two. It took us out of town into vineyard country. We passed row after row of grapes, which appeared to have been recently harvested.

We turned down a lane and drove several hundred yards to what looked like a fancy Kentucky horse barn. Without any explanation, we unloaded and were taken inside and down a flight of steps. When we reached the bottom, we noticed that our two young men in orange jackets had produced guns. They were pointing them at us.

Our joy exploded as they marched us to the end of a long basement and opened a cell. We stepped in without a fight. We were both so deflated that we just stood there. Over their shoulders we could see Regina. She had her head bowed refusing to look our direction. Without a word, she started back up the steps and out of sight. The lights went out and we were left alone in the basement cell. I could hear Rebekah struggling to keep from falling apart in the darkness. I was stunned. I could not have been more off-balance than if I had been kicked squarely in the head by a mule.

Rebekah was the first to speak, "Why would she do this?"

"I don't know. I really don't know."

"I thought that our prayers had been answered. I thought that God had provided a miracle," she said, her voice dripping with disappointment.

"So did I."

As we sat down on the hay-covered floor, there was a long silence. We could hear a heater fan turn on, but it wasn't blowing down into the basement. Instead a chill was creeping through the rock walls.

"What's next?"

"I wish I knew," I said, but I wasn't sure that was true.

"What are they going to do to us?"

I replied, "Every time I think I have it figured out, I'm wrong. I'm sorry, I'm so sorry."

She replied, "Unless I have it confused, I'm the one who has gotten us into this mess. I'm that one who ought to be making apologies."

She snuggled up closer to me and laid her head on my shoulder. We both tried to sleep, but neither of us could. It was impossible to know what time it was, but my guess was that we had been in the basement at least six hours.

About the time we dozed off, we both heard a clang. As we jumped to our feet, the basement lights were turned on. We could hear steps coming down the stairs. Somehow we both recognized the footsteps at the same time.

It was Victor. His laughter was unmistakable. As he walked towards us, he said, "You two couldn't leave well enough alone, could you? You were in an amazing place. Mona is a wonderful cook, right? However, you two had to take the bait."

Standing near the bars, he continued, "In our line of work, we have learned to trust no one. No matter what we pay, anybody can be turned. So we have to test folks from time to time. You two failed, you failed miserably. It's a shame. Nobody organized our book-keeping like you two. You have been a wonderful aid. I'm sorry that it didn't work out. I don't suppose you desire to tell me now where the money is?"

"I've told you before. I don't know about any thirty million dollars. My husband kept this life completely hidden from me. I didn't know about the business, the house, or the money. I don't even know what happened to him," Rebekah rattled off with anger.

Victor smiled and said, "I believe you; I really do, but my guess is that he told you, but you didn't realize it at the time. I think you have the answer to my question, but you simply don't know what you have."

Suddenly he opened the cell door and motioned to Rebekah that a bathroom was under the stairs. She stepped out half expecting for something to happen when she turned her back on us.

Instead Victor said, "We'll be waiting here. Take as long as need."

When she returned, Victor invited me to go take care of my business. When I returned he sat four water bottles on the floor just outside the cell.

As he locked it back, he said, "I've done about all I can do. I'm sorry this is turning out this way. If you can think of anything, it might change how this plays out."

With that he was gone, the lights were out, and we began waiting again.

"I don't know where the money is. I really don't. I don't know why he thinks I do," Rebekah said with passion.

I didn't respond.

"He thinks that I may have it, but not know that I do. How could that be?"

"Perhaps you do?"

With considerable pain in her voice she asked, "What do you mean by that?"

"Don't you remember your business card with the numbers?"

"Yes, but..." she started.

"I have a thought. I wish that I had thought of it sooner. The code is in a particular book, right?" I asked.

"Yes," she said.

"We found a book back at the villa, a book that Gary may have taken great pains to conceal," I said.

"The Bible in the Arabic cover!" she answered.

"Yes, I wish that I had thought about it before. Now I don't know what to do. I fear that it may be too late," I sighed.

"Do we even know where that business card is?" she asked.

"Yes, I think I know where it is; at least where I left it," I said.

"Do you have it?"

"No, not really, but I think I used it as a bookmark in the Bible," I explained.

"Where's the Bible?"

"It's in our bag that we carried with us. I'm guessing that it's upstairs. I don't remember seeing the bag after we were led down here. I'm sure they have gone through it by now," I said.

"Should we ask Victor? Maybe if we show him what we think we have," she said, "I really don't care about the money."

"Do you really think he will just let us go, even if he finds the money?"

She shook her head, "No, he knows we had those names. He knows we were trying to destroy their operation. He can't afford to let us live."

I agreed.

"I wish that I had never gotten you into this mess," she said with sadness.

"I'm not. We may both die tonight, but I wouldn't trade our time together for a single day of life. I love you, Rebekah Black."

"I love you, too, Richard Dempsey."

"I think that both of us knows that, whatever happens, we know too much to really be worried," I said.

"What do you mean?"

"Every time I was about to truly lose my way, He would find me. Every time I was about to just quit... every time I thought that I had lost you...either this has all been a set of weird circumstances, or He really is here, and if He is really here, then we can trust Him now," I said with firmness.

She nodded in agreement.

I continued, "Do you remember me reading to you from the Gospel of John, Chapter 14?"

"Yes, I remember, but I'm not sure which chapter says what. What does Chapter 14 say?"

"In Chapter 14, Jesus said that he was going to go prepare a place for those who loved him—a wonderful place where we will be with him forever."

"If that is true, then..." she said.

I didn't want her to finish the thought, so I finished it for her, "If it's true, then we don't have to be afraid of dying, no fear at all."

CHAPTER 27

Garden of Righteousness

We sat holding each other for at least an hour as the depth of those words pierced our hearts. Eventually, Rebekah said, "When I was in middle school, I was sitting with my grandmother while mom ran some errands. Most of the time, Nana slept, and I didn't really understand all that was wrong with her, but we all knew she was dying. I knew, though I don't think Mom realized I knew.

"I was sitting in a rocking chair by her bed and I must have dozed off. When I awoke, Nana was looking at me with the most amazing smile. Her hand was on my arm. Then Nana said to me, 'My dear, Miss Becky, its beautiful. I have seen it. Don't ever be afraid.' She squeezed my arm and just went to sleep with that amazing smile.

"At the time, watching her die traumatized me. Mom even took me to a psychologist for therapy, but truly it was one of the most special moments I've ever had. I knew that she knew: it must be beautiful."

I leaned over and kissed her forehead.

"There is one thing I wish, however. I wish..." she said but didn't finish.

"What?" I asked.

"I shouldn't say this," she responded.

"What?" I kept asking. Now was the time to be completely transparent.

"You and I both know what is going to happen today or tomorrow, and we're not afraid of that, but I wish that you and I were married. If we're going to die together, I want to be married," she said.

I didn't know what to say.

"I'm sorry, I shouldn't have said that...no I'm not sorry. I'm glad I said it. I want us to be married. You are a preacher. Don't you do weddings?" she asked with some force.

"I can't," I said quietly.

"I know. I was just hoping that maybe..." she said again not quite finishing.

"No, I mean that I can't marry you because I've never asked you," I said.

She turned and looked at me with an amazing expression, but didn't say a word.

"Rebekah, would you accept my hand in marriage? Would you marry me?" I asked.

"Yes, I would Mr. Richard Dempsey. I would love to marry you. As you know, there are times and seasons. Now is certainly the time, but it probably needs to be a short engagement," she said with a wisp of a grin.

I grinned, stood up and helped her to her feet. We both looked like a horrid mess, but the lighting was so dim we couldn't really tell, and besides, it didn't matter.

I took her hands in mine, and started with the words as best that I could remember: "Dearly beloved, we are gathered here together in the sight of God and in the presence of these witnesses to join together this man and this woman in holy matrimony."

I couldn't remember the whole traditional ritual, though I had recited it many times in the past for numerous weddings. The sections that I couldn't recall, I just ad-libbed. When I came to the vows, I said:

"Rebekah, will you have this man, Richard, to be your wedded husband? Will you love him, and keep him for richer for poorer, in sickness and in health, and forsaking all others keep yourself only to him?"

Without hesitation, she shouted, "I do."

I laughed and then repeated the same words for myself, "I, Richard, take you Rebekah..."

I was nearly complete with the ceremony, as best as I could remember, when we heard the door at the top of the stairs unbolt and swing open. Quickly, I said in her ear, "I pronounce that we are husband and wife, and you may kiss the bride."

As I kissed her, the lights came on and footsteps started down the steps.

We stood facing whomever it might be arm in arm. Tears were rolling down Rebekah's cheeks as we saw Victor and two others coming towards us.

"I don't suppose that you have decided to tell me anything of significance," he said almost with a sigh.

"Yes, I think we have," I countered.

He looked surprised, and said, "Really? What would that be?"

"We may have the answer to your question, but we need our bag," I said with certainty.

Without arguing he turned to the man on his left and said, "Go get their bag, and hurry." He trotted off and bounded up the stairs.

"You do realize that the powers that be in our organization are tired of playing games with you. If you truly have something, I'll try to convince them otherwise, but I offer no guarantees at this point," he said.

It didn't take the expressionless man long to return carrying our bag.

Victor unzipped it and peered inside asking what we needed. I told him that there was a book inside with a green Arabic cover. He felt around, but didn't feel it, so he dumped everything out on the floor. The green leather volume was one of the last items to tumble out.

Victor picked it up and looked confused and asked, "You read Arabic?"

We both shook our heads and said, "No."

Victor handed it to the other fellow who was with him, "What does this say?"

He looked at it carefully and said, "It's a classic on Muslim spirituality titled, <u>Riyadh us Saleheen</u>, or in English, <u>Gardens of Righteousness</u> by Imam Nawawi."

"Open it," I commanded.

The assassin did so, and almost jumped backwards as if the book was hot in his hands. He started yelling, "It's been defaced; it's been butchered."

He quickly tossed it back to Victor who opened it and glanced at the pages. He, too, was greatly surprised, "This is a Bible! Are you trying to make us into clowns?"

"No," I responded, "Do you see a business card tucked inside?"

He hastily thumbed through it and yelled, "No!" Then he tossed it through the bars to me. "Take it with you. You're going to need it where you're going." He looked as cruel as we had ever seen him. I tried to argue, but even after I scanned for the business card, it wasn't to be found.

With that he turned and left. The other two motioned for us to back away from the cell door. They clearly had a job to perform and were all business. Once we had taken a few steps backward, they opened the cell door and asked us to step forward. Very few words were said. They marched us up the stairs, through the house, and into the garage where we saw a van with darkened windows. We were told to climb into the middle seat. One of the two climbed in behind us holding an automatic rifle. The other took the driver's seat. They didn't seem to think that it was necessary to tie our hands.

Within minutes we were out of the city and passing through the rural countryside of Sicily. We both knew what their intentions were, but neither of us had any idea how to frustrate their plans. I could hear an old voice in my memory saying, "Relax and allow the inevitable," but I could also hear a much older voice saying, "Trust me, simply trust me."

After riding for about a half hour, the van stopped at an intersection as several dozen vehicles were coming towards us. We evidently were turning left when the traffic cleared. Looking down our intended destination, I could see that the road was very narrow and lined with a rock fence on either side. In a way it reminded me of many of the rural roads of Kentucky.

When the last of the traffic passed, we did indeed turn left. In less than a half-mile we had to stop again. An old man in a wagon loaded with hay, pulled by a couple of oxen, had some wheel trouble. The bearded old man was attempting to repair the wagon wheel, but he had the road completely blocked. At first our driver was angry, yelling obscenities out the window, but strangely enough that didn't relieve the situation. At last he exited and offered to help the old man, seeing how there was little choice.

Rebekah and I could do nothing except sit and watch, and wait our turn. The guard seated behind us stayed alert. It took at least fifteen minutes for our driver and old man to repair the wagon wheel. It was now approaching dusk. Low cast clouds had the countryside boxed in and dreary. I prayed that the wagon would never be repaired, but that prayer wasn't answered.

As the wagon started, our driver began walking back towards our van. Just as he stepped back into the driver's seat, our van lunged forward with a massive shock. Someone had slammed into us from behind. The van seemed to have resisted any extensive damage, but the little pickup that rammed us was crushed. Both of our chaperones sprang into action and exited the van with shouts of anger and frustration. Rebekah and I could see out the back window. The driver of the pickup didn't seem to be moving at all with his head down on the steering wheel.

The van door was left standing open. Was this our opportunity? With both guards checking out the other driver and the damage done, we could make a break. What's the worst that could happen? However, just as I started to move, Rebekah had her hand on my leg shaking her head, "No, no, wait."

Before I could argue, I heard popping sounds. The guard who had been seated behind us was immediately down clutching his shoulder. He was looking wildly around for the direction of his attackers. More shots were fired, and he doubled over. Knowing his time was limited; he looked directly through the back of the van, aimed and fired. The van's back window just exploded. He was still pulling the trigger when he went down for good.

The van driver was crouching down between the pickup's door and the slumped over driver of the wrecked truck. He was returning fire randomly, but shots continued to pepper his position from various directions. I had my eyes just barely up over the back seat when I saw the driver of the pickup slowly rise. He reached under his jacket and produced a pistol. He and our driver simultaneously exchanged shots from close range.

"I think both are down. We need to get out of here," I shouted, but there was no response. Rebekah was slumped down in the floorboard of the van with her head lying on the seat. Blood was everywhere. She was just barely conscious, gripping her shoulder. I started applying pressure on the wound, but I could not discern whether there were multiple wounds. It looked like the bullet had passed through her shoulder with both an entrance and exit.

She looked up at me in the dim lighting of the van's dome light, and said, "Getting shot doesn't hurt as bad as I thought it would. Are you hurt?"

"No," I said almost feeling guilty.

CHAPTER 28

Die Hard

W ithin seconds there were three men around us. One was checking on the status of the driver of the pickup. Another was helping me climb out, while the other was checking on Rebekah from the other door. He seemed to know exactly what he was doing. I didn't have much choice but to let him.

Within ten minutes a military truck pulled in behind us. Rebekah was loaded onto a stretcher. Once she was in the truck, they started an IV and were giving her meds for the pain. All of her vitals were strong. The driver that rammed the back of the van had taken a shot through the chest. He obviously wasn't faring well. They had laid him on a stretcher at the foot of the ambulance, and were working on him as quickly as they could. The look on their faces revealed professionalism, but also hopelessness.

One of the men approached me, calling for another stretcher. I argued with him that I was unhurt, but he wasn't buying it. I was covered in blood, but he soon discovered most of it was from Rebekah. I did have a cut above the right eye that had bled profusely, but I couldn't even feel it.

I felt the urge to pray for the truck driver and Rebekah both, but as I started I heard a voice. The driver of the pickup was trying to speak. He simply said, "Tell Rebekah I'm sorry. I'm so very sorry." With that he relaxed. His breathing stopped. It was over.

Rebekah's eyes popped wide open when I looked back down at her. She barely spoke, "He's gone, isn't he?"

I nodded.

"He gave himself for us," she added.

I nodded again.

"I know his voice," she said.

I looked confused, but didn't say a word.

"That's Gary. That's my husband," she said.

All I could do was hold her hand.

In less than an hour we pulled into the US Naval Air Station Sigonella, Sicily. We drove straight to the hospital, which was about ten miles from the actual base. Rebekah was unloaded and taken into the emergency staging area. A nurse challenged whether I should stay, but I explained that she was my wife. Rebekah smiled when she heard my proclamation, but I did have to step aside while the medical team evaluated the wound.

An x-ray revealed what I had assumed. A small fragment of the bullet was still lodged in her shoulder, but it had not done any serious damage. She was taken to surgery within minutes. About an hour and half later, I was invited into recovery.

While I waited, a nurse treated the cut over my eye and cleaned up my face. As she completed her task, one of the men who rescued us came in and sat down beside me. He wanted to tell me something, but seemed to hesitate. At last he confessed.

"Regina is very sorry about what she did to you two. She was scared. She was afraid that someone might be hurt if she didn't carry out their proposal," he said.

"Is she okay?"

"Not really. Physically she is recovering, but they broke her jaw. Somehow, they thought she knew where the money would be, since Rebekah didn't."

"I'm confused—she helped us escape, and then turned us in, right?"

"I know, and she wants me to tell you that she is very sorry. As you well know, they have a way of putting terrible pressure upon a person. She cracked. She was terrified," he explained.

"Was she afraid that they would kill her?"

"No, that wouldn't have scared her. She would have given her life for the two of you. She is a special woman."

"So what terrified her?"

"She did it to protect me."

"You? Who are you?"

"I'm José. I'm Regina's son. They convinced her that they had me. They broke her through fear of losing me."

"I understand, I really do understand. It's one thing to stand up for what's right when you only have your life to give, but when it involves the one you love...you can be broken. I know that." He left before I was called into the recovery room.

When I entered she was awake. They hadn't needed to put her under a general anesthesia, so she was aware, but somewhat looped. She grabbed my hand and whispered rather hoarsely, "I think we need to tell Him thanks."

I nodded in agreement and we both offered a prayer of thanksgiving. It was a simple, but sincere prayer of gratitude. Both of us were crying when the nurse checked in on us, but we told her that all was good, and we meant it.

The nurse explained, "The doctors recommend that you wait a few days before you try to travel. We recommend that you stay here on base. That way, the doctors are close and you'll still be safe, but some of the upper staff from some weird organization with multiple letters wants to visit with you when you're healthy and caught up on your sleep."

"We would love to visit with them," we both agreed.

The hospital food really wasn't bad. It didn't compare to Mona's, but then nobody compared to Mona, but the Sicilian pasta with sun-dried tomatoes and olives, along with a fresh salad, was enjoyable. As I helped unroll the napkin for Rebekah, she said, "Quite a honeymoon adventure wouldn't you say?"

I responded, "It will be difficult to explain this little adventure to anyone. We will need to invent some agreed-upon story to tell others years from now. If we told the whole truth, people would think we were hallucinating."

After we finished our pastries, we turned on the television. We were both exhausted and just needed to watch something that would take us away from reality. Nearly all the stations were Italian, but there was a CNN station, and then an America movie channel with Italian subtitles. Believe it or not, it was showing *Die Hard* with Bruce Willis. We watched about fifteen minutes of the movie before we looked at each other and shook our heads. When guns go off in real life, fear and adrenaline kick in, and there's no time for witty humor. We shut it off.

After the nurse came in and checked out the shoulder, I sat down on the side of the bed, rubbing Rebekah's foot through the sheet.

"I feel bad forcing you into a shotgun wedding," she confessed.

"What do you mean?"

"We were both under duress. Perhaps we should reconsider the marriage deal," she explained.

"Is that what you want to do?"

She paused a long time before answering, "No, I want to be married, and I want to be married to you. But if you would prefer, we can back off and do it right later; you know, the normal way with friends and family, a ring, a white cake, and maybe even a license."

I thought for a moment before saying, "If we waited, got a license, had a ceremony with a 'real' preacher, and drank some punch, would we be any more married than we are now?"

She didn't respond.

I continued, "Do you consider yourself married right now?"

She still didn't answer. She was afraid to give the wrong answer and perhaps put more pressure on me.

"Do you think God considers us married right now?" I asked.

That triggered a response, and she said with authority, "Yes, I do."

"So do I. In case you don't know it, I love you, Mrs. Dempsey. This is our time and our season," I said.

She was crying.

Neither of us realized fully what the nurse meant when she had been in earlier. She said that the doctor was going to give Rebekah something to help her sleep. What we didn't understand is that she had already added those meds through the IV. With tears of joy flowing, she just drifted away. I sat beside her at least an hour, just studying her face as she slept. What a woman! She barely cried when she was shot, but for me to confirm our marriage, she cried like a baby.

As I sat beside her bed, the blood pressure monitor was standing almost eye level with me. On the back of it was the tiny imprint of a lion silhouette. With nothing but the usual sounds of the hospital, my eyes focused upon the small image. I thought about the cardboard image of the lion in the truck that *ran* along side us. I thought about the concrete beast that had become our personal companion standing beside the swimming pool. I thought about the touch on the shoulder on the ship. I thought...

Leaving her, I went to find a telephone. I couldn't imagine what my daughters were thinking. They would be going through what Rebekah went through for four years. The head nurse took me to a doctor's lounge. She knew the situation and knew that I didn't even have an ID, much less a credit card. She handed me a pass code and told me that I could call any where in the world using that code.

I thanked her, sat down, and picked up the phone. As I started to dial I froze. I couldn't remember my daughters' phone numbers. For years, I just punched a button on my cell phone and their phones would ring, but now I couldn't remember my own number, much less theirs. Finally, I called the operator and directory assistance to get my own daughters' numbers. It has been almost a year. I almost felt guilty for not calling before, but it wasn't like I had much choice. The line rang.

"Hello," my older daughter Lisa answered.

"Honey, it's Dad," I said.

"Dad, oh my, where are you? We thought...we've called the police...Dad...we were afraid," she blurted out her emotions.

"I'm sorry, I'm so sorry. I have been held hostage, but we're free now. I think we are coming home in a day or so. Honey, I have missed you. I'm so sorry. I wish that there had been some way to let you know that I was alive. I can't imagine what you and Micah have gone through," I said.

"Dad, are you hurt? Where are you?" Lisa asked.

I said, "Right now we're at a Naval hospital in Sicily, but we're good."

"Who is 'we'? Who are you with?" Lisa asked.

"Honey, it's a long story, but we're good. I can tell you all about it when we get home, but yes, I'm not alone. Honey, I got remarried," I said realizing how strange this all sounded.

"What? You were held hostage and got married?" she asked.

"I know it sounds unbelievable, but you will like her. I'll explain it all when we get home," I said, "I can't wait to see you."

"We can't wait, either. It's been a long time. Micah has some exciting news to share with you."

When I called Micah, she broke down and cried when she heard my voice. I explained it all as best I could, but she just kept crying. After she finally calmed down, she gave me her news. She and John were pregnant. I hung up with a big grin on my face. I was going to be granddad.

CHAPTER 29

North Star

The next morning a nurse awakened me as I slept in a chair in Rebekah's room. She checked Rebekah's bandage and moved her arm gently. Evidently the arm was stiff and painful, because she moaned.

"I'll bring you two some breakfast, but we have been told that there are some folks who would like to visit with you when you feel up to it."

A couple of nurses helped Rebekah with a shower, and then we had some cold eggs and toast, but food didn't matter. The nurse insisted on a wheelchair, though Rebekah argued. I rolled her down the hall to a meeting room. Two men and a woman stood to greet us.

After brief introductions, Ms. Melinda Thompson began by saying, "You two have been through a great deal. We are all so thrilled that you have survived. We trust that your arm is feeling better today."

Rebekah nodded with a big smile and assured them all that she was feeling much better. The shower and hair wash had done the trick more than the morning meds.

"You two have seen and experienced much that might help us track down and break this particular criminal organization. We understand that both copies of your files were confiscated and lost, but if you can help us from what you remember, it might be of great assistance."

"I don't want to be rude, but who are you again? Who do you represent? What organization do you work for?" I said with a touch of fire in my eyes.

They looked at each other and nodded. Ms. Thompson said, "I work for the Polaris Project. It's a nonprofit organization seeking to end modern slavery. Polaris, as you probably know, is the North Star. The Underground Railroad instructed slaves to follow Polaris to their freedom, back before the Civil War. We operate in a similar spirit.

"Larry, to my left, works for the United Nations Global Initiative to Fight Human Trafficking, or UN-GIFT as we call it. Bill, to my right, is working with the Department of Homeland Security under the authority of the Office to Monitor and Combat Trafficking in Persons."

Both men nodded and smiled.

"However, we all work unofficially for a shadowy organization that gives us the opportunity to do whatever it takes to stop this blight in the international community. We would prefer that you not ask for additional details about that aspect, but it gives us certain unrestricted liberties, such as staging the black ops rescue operation that brought you out of harm's way. Aren't you glad we didn't have to wait a couple of hours for approval from some government bureaucracy before we could move to help you two?"

I nodded with understanding and approval, as did Rebekah.

"So what can you tell us? What do you remember that you had on those lost files?" Ms. Thompson asked.

"You're right – both discs were taken, as was my laptop, but I still have a zip drive with the information," I blurted out. All of their eyes lit up with delight, including Rebekah's.

"However, the last time I did this we were nearly eliminated. How can I know that you are who you say your are?" I said with firmness. My challenge to them caught them all off guard. It was very unexpected even to me.

Ms. Thompson asked, "What would it take to convince you that we are who we say we are?"

"We're on a US Naval base in Sicily, right?" I asked.

"Yes," Ms. Thompson affirmed.

"Ask the base Commander to come see us and tell us that he knows who you three are," I said.

Ms. Thompson nodded her head and said, "I'm almost certain that the CO hasn't returned from the States, but there is a visiting Air Force Colonel on base who knows us well. We'll see if we can locate him and invite him in for a visit. Will that suffice?"

I nodded in agreement.

One of the aides hung up the phone and said, "Colonel Brighton said he would be here in fifteen minutes. He wanted to meet you two anyway."

While we waited, I asked, "Where is Regina?"

Ms. Thompson said, "Her jaw is wired up, but she is down the hall. She has been very uncomfortable, but she would like to see you whenever possible."

Rebekah asked, "Where is Gary's body?"

Ms. Thompson hesitated, but finally answered, "He's here at the hospital, but we are unsure what we are to do. His records indicate that you are still his next of kin. Perhaps we should ask you what should be done."

Rebekah said, "I'll let you know about that. Gary apparently embezzled some money from the organization. They think I know where the cash is, but I don't. Do you know anything about this money?"

"No, we know nothing about it. Gary joined our organization only for a short time. We didn't know whether we could trust him, so we kept a very close watch. He never mentioned any such funds," said Ms. Thompson.

Eventually Colonel Brighton entered the room. Two lower officers accompanied him. He went straight to Rebekah, and said, "I trust that you are feeling better." He shook my hand, and then said after taking a seat, "How may I help you?"

"I turned over information about this human trafficking organization yesterday to what appeared to be legitimate individuals. That trust nearly got us killed. I have no reason to not trust these good people, but this is too important. Do you know them?" I asked as I pointed to Melinda, Larry and Bill.

"Yes, I know Mr. Larry Brown sitting there to your right. He has been with UN-GIFT for several years. He has always struck me as being serious and effective. I trust him completely as a special ops engineer."

Pointing to the other man, he continued, "Bill Reynolds is CIA, and I'm not sure you should trust any spook." Everybody relaxed and laughed, but he continued, "Bill's a good man and a patriot."

After clearing his throat, he continued, "Ms. Thompson is retired black ops. She has been extremely helpful to my family several times over the years." He leaned back in his chair and nodded for the two lower officers to step outside.

When the door closed, he said, "Four years ago my daughter was on a mission trip to Bolivia with our church. They were helping young women in the jungle to understand the importance of knowing who they were as individuals in Christ. During the night, my daughter and four of the girls that were sleeping together in a hut were abducted. We believe that all five of the girls traveled across the Andes and eventually were loaded onto an oil tanker off the coast of Argentina. That's where the trail went cold. It's been nearly four years now, and we have yet to receive any other information. I have visited with Melinda Thompson several times over the years concerning this foul business. I will vouch for her."

Then he turned to Melinda and said, "Whatever I can do for you and Polaris just let me know." With that he stood, shook our hands, and exited the hospital meeting room.

I looked at Melinda and said, "The zip drive has been rolled up in the back of my underwear until last night, but I think it's unharmed. It's in my pocket now."

I handed the flash drive to the man nearest me, the one named Bill. He immediately inserted it into his laptop. It loaded. He then sent it to several e-mails as an attachment, and then handed it back to me. A printer across the room fired up and began to print a hard copy.

I said, "How long do you think it will take before you can start busting these guys? They are dangerous, very dangerous."

Melinda said, "We're going to move as soon as possible, but as you know this is a complex and massive organization. When we strike, we need to be able to strike swiftly and accurately."

"What about Victor and the house here in Sicily where we were held?" Rebekah asked.

"We've already been there. The house was vacated. They were probably gone within minutes of your rescue. When your two assassins didn't check in, they disappeared immediately. With your information, we hope we can zero in and locate them. I can't stress how important this is," she said, "and by the way, we found your bag, but not your laptop. We'll bring it by the room."

"What about Victor?" I asked.

"What about him?" she responded.

"We have been with him in Argentina, Tunisia, and now in Sicily. It looks like he would be fairly easy to find," I asserted.

"Yes, but if we take him down now, we may miss the top tier of the organization. We need the Victors, but there are others up the food chain that we must attempt to identify. Without the head the body will grow new legs," she outlined.

Rebekah asked, "Can I see Regina?"

Ms. Thompson nodded, "Yes, I think that can be arranged. We'll need to check to be sure she is ready and able."

The nurse came about an hour after we returned to the room. I rolled Rebekah down the hall to Regina's room. She was sitting up on the side of the bed. Her face was swollen and a wire harness was holding her jaw in place. There was bruising all over her face and arms.

When she saw Rebekah in the wheelchair, she started crying. In a muffled whisper she said, "I'm so sorry. Please forgive me. I feel absolutely horrible."

"We understand why. I met your son. He explained it to me. If anyone understands how devious and diabolical the organization is, we do. We forgive you," I said.

"You talked with my son? They made me believe that they would hurt him. I'm so sorry," Regina said.

Tears were running down both of our faces. Rebekah said, "We know. We forgive you."

We tried a group hug, but with slings, wheel-chairs and wire harnesses, it was more like a gentle three-way pat on the back. My love for people never really left. It had been just hibernating.

When we returned to Rebekah's room our duffle bag was sitting in the chair. A quick survey revealed that the few clothes we had were still there, our phones were there without their SIM cards, and even our passports were still tucked away behind the secret flap. The doctor checked on the shoulder late in the afternoon. He was pleased with the progress and asked if we wanted to go home. A military transport was leaving in the morning, and we were welcome to board if we desired. We accepted the invitation.

Chapter 30

Welcome Home

The flight back to the States was the first time that Rebekah and I had any time to start talking about what marriage meant for us. Did I want to move to Boston, or did she want to move to Lexington? Neither of us was thinking straight. We were both so emotionally exhausted and just spinning around in a daze. The one constant was that we both loved each other and had no regrets about out marriage. Other than that, very little was clear in our thinking. It took us several days to come close to acting normal, whatever that was.

My daughters threw a "welcome home/wedding announcement" party, and it was enjoyable to introduce Rebekah to many of my old friends from Lexington and my past congregation, although the situation was strange for most of them. The abbreviated story that we agreed upon left many still asking questions, and I could sense that though there were many smiles and hugs to our faces, behind our backs were rumors and questions. I really couldn't blame them. Being held hostage, but being set free as a married couple sounded weird.

I even felt that way when we attended worship. It was interesting for both of us because the preacher's message was on the three men in the fiery furnace, and how in all of our trials in life, the Lord would be with us. We both resisted the temptation to laugh out loud, not because we thought it was silly, but because we knew it to be more than true.

On top of those feelings of being talked about, Rebekah and I struggled with our own emotions. There were times when one or both of us would just break down into tears. Rebekah's shoulder had healed without issue, and with some physical therapy she regained a full range of motion. However, there were nights when one or both of us would wake up screaming in terror.

We visited a counselor one afternoon, but realized after a few minutes that if we told him everything that had happened, he would assume that we both had lost our minds. We limited the story to the shooting and the fear of dying, and he offered some helpful advice on solving problems with life after a crisis. Mostly what he said was that we needed to talk about the event with someone who understood. We both agreed. It helped that we both understood each other, but neither of us really understood ourselves. We spent most of our time in Lexington by Rebekah's choice, but I had a growing sense that we didn't belong there, either. Her business associate wanted to buy out Rebekah's share of the furniture business, which was a good thing. Her Boston apartment sold within weeks of being on the market.

We secured a marriage license, but decided that the vows in Tunisia were valid in our hearts and before God.

She did close out the UPS mailbox, but she left the bank account at Boston City Bank open. With the sale of the business she was comfortable financially, but she didn't know what to do with the two million that remained in Gary's old account.

After six weeks of being home, we received a phone call. It was Ms. Thompson from the Polaris Project, though we had already been tipped off by a Fox News report that something had happened which struck a blow to one of the largest international human trafficking organizations. She informed us that over sixty "key associates" had been arrested. Victor resisted and died with multiple gunshots. Four oil tanker captains would be going to prison. Two others had disappeared.

Her last news flash was the one that struck me the deepest. A man had been found frozen to death in a cabin on the Baca Grande Estancia. It was still unknown as to exactly what happened. There was no food in his cabin, so he may have starved to death. The snows were four feet deep, but she explained that it happened in another canyon about twenty miles to the South from our place of confinement. That news item left me speechless.

She paused for a moment to let me process before continuing, "When the man was discovered, we believed we had found Gary's brother Garrett, but DNA testing has proven that not to be the case. Garrett's whereabouts are still unknown."

Rebekah and I never did feel a bitterness or hatred toward Victor, but we didn't excuse him either. What he had done to us was beyond brutal, but in our hearts we had discovered forgiveness towards him. However, when Ms. Thompson informed us that he had been killed in a gun battle, we both found a measure of healing. Knowing that at least Victor would never do to another what he had done to us gave us a measure of peace. Neither of us ever woke up in screams and sweats again.

It's hard to describe the nature of faith and how the adventure changed us. For example, it's one thing to say you believe in Bigfoot on the basis that such a critter could be living in the wilderness, and maybe you have found an oversized footprint. However, there is a different level to your belief if your tent was ripped wide open and you stared face to face with Sasquatch. In a way, that's how we felt. We believed that God loved us before our experience, but once we had been "touched," faith took on a whole new meaning.

Believe it or not, Rebekah and I never discussed the thirty million. There was nothing we could do about it. We still had the Arabic covered Bible, but Rebekah's business card with Gary's code was lost. When we tried to offer it to Victor it wasn't there, and it hadn't fallen out into our duffle bag. Without it there was little to talk about. We didn't even know what the code would have told us. A couple of times, I tried to remember the numbers from our tent experience, but there was no way. Too much water had gone under the bridge.

Several months later, after supper, I picked up the little Arabic book titled the *Gardens of Righteousness* and turned to the Gospel of John. Reading those words and "reliving" those stories had literally renewed my life on that special day at the villa. The "touch" on the beach and in the ship's cell were becoming distant memories, but that afternoon with the Word was still so alive I could almost taste it.

Even the vision of the angel, or Jesus himself, or maybe the Lion—we could never decide—which Rebekah saw on the fake torture videos seemed like a decade ago. But standing on the porch at the cabin, knowing that we weren't alone and reading the Gospel of John in the villa were both as real and vibrant as if they had happened yesterday. As I reflected about those memories, I thumbed through the book. It wasn't the first time I had looked through it. Probably I had done so at least a dozen times since we left Sicily, but this time I stopped at the last page. I read those last few lines:

He who testifies to these things says,
"Yes, I am coming soon."
Amen, Come, Lord Jesus.
The grace of the Lord Jesus be with God's people.
Amen.

The words had a power, "The grace will be with God's people." The grace will be with me. As I contemplated that amazing truth, I flipped the next page over, which was really a blank page from the original Arabic book. There nestled between the pages was Rebekah's business card. How I had not found it before was amazing, but there it was.

Rebekah was sitting up reading in bed when I entered the room. Without saying a word, I turned off the light to her mild protest, grabbed a tiny flashlight, and crawled under the covers making a "tent" as we did before to conceal our voices from the microphone in Tunisia. She giggled and asked what I had in mind, but grew silent when I held up the green leather Arabic book titled *Gardens of Righteousness*. In dramatic fashion I opened it to the last page and produced the business card, *Rebekah Black, Upscale Furniture and Fine Décor.*

"Are you ready for some code breaking? Shall I read the code and you find the reference?"

She responded, "Yes, but are you sure this is the right book?"

"No, but let's plan to celebrate either way," I said with a wink, "Ready?"

"104-47-1."

It took her a minute to count down 47 rows, but finally, "Hundred." It says, "Hundred."

"267-5-10."

"Foot."

"105-2-7."

"North."

"121-4-9."

"Believe it or not, it says 1775, do you think it's referring to a year?" she asked.

I didn't know.

"83-12-8."

"West."

"104-11-3."

"That's the number sixteen."

"104-46-8."

"Same page let me count. It says 'south,' I think," she said with mounting excitement.

"200-5-5."

"Seven."

"83-12-8."

"It says 'West' again. Where are we?" she asked.

"If I have it accurate so far, it says, '100 foot north, 1775 west, 16 south, and then 7 west.' These are directions," I said with even more excitement. "Let's continue."

"100-11-1."

"Three."

"96-31-10."

"Stones."

"6-25-5."

"It says, 'Began' if I counted right," she said.

"1382-14-14."

"Barns."

"We have: 100 foot north, 1775 west, 16 south, then 7 west, three stones, began barns," I read.

"Does that make any sense to you?" Rebekah asked.

"Maybe. Victor was certain that Gary hid the money at the house near Bajo Los Caracoles. That's why there was a backhoe digging holes all around," I said.

"The barn, the old barn didn't burn," she said.

"Yes, I think you're right. North of the barn would be down towards the river. West would be up along the river. Going south would take us back off the river, and then seven more steps West. Then we look for three stones. Wow," I breathed.

"Sounds to me like somebody needs to go back to Argentina, but I'm not sure that you're well enough," she said with a grin of pure joy.

"Me not well enough? I'll probably need to make this trip alone considering your physical therapy," I said.

She said, "Don't even think about it. I'll show you what is well enough," and she switched off the flashlight.

The next morning we outlined our plans. The thought of going back to Argentina alone didn't set well with either of us, but the thought of not going wasn't an option. Eventually we called Melinda Thompson at Polaris. I explained our discovery of the code and our conclusion, without bluntly telling her where exactly we thought the money was. As we talked I wondered it she even knew how much Gary's embezzled funds might be. She asked how she could help.

I said, "This will sound self centered, but if we find the money, whose is it?"

She replied, "We may need to confirm Argentina law, but my suspicion is that if it's rediscovered on your personal property and no one else has a claim on it, then it belongs to you. Even if it's not on your property, and no one has a claim, then I still believe that it's yours."

"How does the Polaris Project receive it's funding?" I asked.

She answered, "We receive some government grants, some UN funds, some ill gotten booty we have confiscated, and considerable private funding."

"If you help us find it, protect us, and help us get it home, there may be a sizable gift to the Polaris Project. Of course, I will need to visit with Rebekah," I said.

"Such a gift would be greatly appreciated, but with or without a gift to Polaris, I would suggest you not return alone. We rounded up every individual we could, but several disappeared on us. We also have several government types being watched. We would be willing to help you in any way possible, because you have already helped us in such a major way," she said.

Since she had some other issues she was involved with, she suggested that we all might meet in Argentina. Meeting in Buenos Aires seemed to be the most convenient for everyone. The Polaris Project would have air travel arranged to take us out on the Pampas to Bajo Los Caracoles.

"Do you really think this might be...?" Rebekah started.

"I don't know what to think. I just know that I'm thrilled to be going back to the place where I fell in love with the most wonderful woman I've ever known."

"You are a hopeless romantic," she said and kissed me.

Our last flight together across Patagonia was exactly fifteen months ago to the day. It seemed bizarre to think that over a year of our lives had been stolen by the past events, but we both knew in our hearts that we wouldn't exchange that year for anything.

The unmarked Lear jet provided by Polaris was certainly a step up from that earlier flight, but I wondered if the pilot understood the nature of the runway at Bajo Los Caracoles; however, I decided that such was not my worry. Nor did I comment on Ms. Thompson's report that we all had reservations at Hotel Bajo Caracoles. I just hoped that Victoria had completed the remodeling project. I also was secretly hoping that she had a new batch of her special strawberry jam.

Victoria was delighted to see Rebekah and me, and the remodeling did seem to be complete. Melinda, Larry, and Bill seemed to take it all in stride. Each of them had been in far worse places. We did use Victoria's rental, though it was a different vehicle. She explained that the green Citroen had burned up when Regina's house burned and that the insurance company replaced it with a red Fiat several years newer. It would easily hold all five of us.

Victoria hesitated at first to ask, but finally admitted that from the town gossip, she learned that Rebekah was the heir to the burned out house and property and, thus, the rightful owner to the mail in Box 18. We both immediately glanced up at the box and noticed two letters in the slot. She explained that the law required that the rental on the post office box needed to be paid up to date before she could "deliver" the mail.

We both laughed and asked what was owed. On her archaic calculator she started punching in numbers and then even more numbers. Finally it printed out the results and she reported, "In American, $17 dollars." I handed her a twenty and told her to keep the change. She handed Rebekah the two letters. Both letters were from an Argentinean Insurance company completely in Spanish. Victoria helped us translate their meanings, but they both were asking to whom they should forward the insurance check. We told Victoria that we would take care of that.

CHAPTER 31

Counting Steps

The five of us found the lane down to the River house easily, though it appeared to be considerably less visible. Clearly, little traffic had been down this road over the last year. The backhoe and portable toilets were gone, but some of the holes the backhoe created remained. The ashen square where the house once stood was still readily apparent, but spots of grass were growing over it. The barn, however, looked as it always had. We didn't even open the door. The faint trail down from the corner of the old barn down to the river was still discernible.

We both counted independently the hundred steps north towards the river. That took us to the river's edge. Then we started counting 1775 steps upstream which took us due west. We left marks in the sand every three hundred feet just in case we lost count. Ms. Thompson confirmed our counting with her GPS unit. Then we counted out the next sixteen steps and then the final seven. We were standing on a sand bank that appeared to once have been the bank to the river before it doubled back, leaving this bank dry and abandoned.

At the top of the sand bar were three rocks, large but moveable once we dug the sand out from around them. The sand was dry and with our bare hands we could dig fairly easily. About a foot deep under the position of the three stones, I discovered the top of a PVC pipe. It had a cap sealing it, but neither the cap nor the pipe would move no matter how hard I pulled. I began to think the pipe might have been twenty feet long, extending straight downward into concrete. Larry and Bill tried to help but we didn't make any progress.

I thought that I remembered seeing some garden tools back in the barn, so Larry and I walked back to see what we could discover. We needed a shovel at least. Rebekah, Melinda, and Bill would wait for us, but at the last minute, Bill decided to walk with us. In the barn I found a forked garden spade, but that was all. I hoped that would be enough. When we returned we found the two women sitting back down by the river. Instead of jumping up and joining us, they signaled us to come join them.

"What's up?" I asked.

"Do you remember the first time we saw the house and barn?" Rebekah asked.

"Sure, that first morning we met Regina. You talked her into letting us stay at the house. I was impressed," I replied.

"No, before that. We drove on past and looked back from the overlook on the road. We could see the house and barn from a distance," Rebekah said.

I said, "Yes, I remember, but what does that matter?"

"We're being watched from up there now," Melinda said.

"Are you serious?" I said.

"I saw a flash in the sun, but when I started really watching, I have seen at least two people on the ledge. They're still there. They are watching to see what we are doing," said Melinda.

I stood and casually looked up towards the ledge. Sure enough there was someone standing there and perhaps the top of a vehicle.

"What do you think we should do?" I asked.

"Probably it's just a tourist, but to be sure let's pretend to walk back towards the house. There's a big boulder about 200 yards back up the river that we can all disappear behind. From there we can watch what they do," suggested Melinda. We all agreed without another viable plan.

Casually we walked back along the river. I left the spade fork by the river. When we rounded the boulder we just sat down. From the overlook perspective we hoped it would look like we had continued to the house area knowing they wouldn't be able to see us. Behind the rock I found a tiny crack that I could peep through up to the overlook. After about five minutes, two figures appeared, and then both disappeared. We sat there at least another hour, but no one reappeared.

We knew we had found something, but we really didn't know what. We assumed it would be cash, probably rolled up in the PVC, but we hadn't thought through the situation. Neither of us mentioned to our trio of Polaris guides the amount that we had been told Gary embezzled. We dared not mention such a total even to ourselves.

After we were convinced that we weren't being observed from above any longer, we decided to continue trying to remove the PVC pipe. The spade fork broke up the wet sand, and eventually we were able to wiggle the pipe loose. It was only two feet long, but was surprisingly heavy. That's why it had been so difficult to pull out. As it finally slipped out, the sight of several more tubes became visible.

I suspected its contents almost immediately, but until I could pry off the cap I couldn't be sure. I slammed the spade fork against the cap several times before it popped off. It was exactly what I expected. It was full of gold bullion coins: Krugerrands, Maple Leafs and American Eagles to be precise.

My mind was spinning, two feet of one-ounce gold coins; how many coins would fit into two feet? I didn't know, but if the tube weighed twenty-five pounds, with gold at $1,700 per ounce, then one tube would be worth...nearly $700,000 dollars.

The spade fork continued probing into the sand. Every other probe discovered another tube. In all we discovered forty-eight sealed pipes. Assuming each consisted of about the same as the first, we had a pile that was worth at least $34 million. We continued to spade the area in a circle around to be sure we weren't walking away from several more such tubes, but we found no additional deposits. Our "friends" from above never reappeared either. It took us several trips to carry the forty-eight loaded tubes to the rental Fiat van. Stacking them under the back seat caused the van to sink down on its axle.

Larry and Bill decided that they wouldn't need the rest of us for the last trip. I wasn't so certain, but Larry insisted, so the two of them left to bring back the remainder of the tubes. The moment the two were out of sight, Melinda's face changed, showing worry. She had clearly gone on alert. Seeing her transform, I asked if she thought there was a problem. She didn't respond. She was concerned, and didn't care about showing us that she was. She started checking the time as if she were late for a meeting.

After Larry and Bill had been gone for slightly over fifteen minutes, Melinda starting walking towards the barn. Rebekah and I stood beside the van alone still wondering what had her so concerned. Within a few minutes Larry came walking up the path carrying three of the pipes cradled like a baby. He was by himself. As he passed the barn, Melinda walked up behind him with her gun drawn.

She asked, "Where's Bill?"

Larry didn't turn around, but simply said, "He's behind me; he just couldn't keep up," but as he spoke he smoothly dropped the weighted tubes and drew a pistol from under his jacket and attempted to reel around. He didn't fully make it. One shot from Melinda's Glock echoed around the canyon walls, and clutching his chest, Larry slumped to the ground.

Rebekah and I both dropped to the ground behind the van. There was no place to hide, and we had no reason to think that Melinda didn't have us in her sights next. We could see her feet under the vehicle, walking towards us and around the van, but instead of firing her weapon, she asked if we were unharmed. We nodded.

"Come, let's go check on Bill," she said as she replaced her firearm.

We both stood to our feet, but were completely confused as we followed her. As we passed by Larry, it was clear that he would not be going anywhere.

Following the trail back down to the river, she told us they had been notified that it was possible that Larry Brown had been bought out. The phone call cast the suspicion and tipped the agency to the possibility. She informed us that she and Bill had made an arrangement. He would never be far behind Larry. If the two of them weren't together, then Larry had tried to take him out, and would be dangerous. Neither Rebekah nor I knew what to say, but once we were down to the river's edge we all started jogging. When we passed the boulder where we hid from the watchers above, we found Bill lying at the water's edge.

As first Rebekah and I assumed the worse, but the closer we got, the more we saw that Bill was alive and moving. We rushed to his side. It appeared that he had been shot, from the three holes in his shirt, but there was no blood. His Kevlar vest had stopped all three of the bullets, but he was still somewhat out of breath.

"What happened?" I asked with considerable excitement.

"He helped me load the pipe sections, then as I turned he shot me. I'm going to be sore," he said. Melinda helped him to his feet, and they started to walk back towards the house site.

Rebekah and I stood there, still stunned by the events, and watched as they moved outside of earshot.

"Your heart is racing," she leaned over and said in a hush tone.

"So is yours," I added.

"This is an ugly business," she said as we started to follow them, having picked up the two remaining tubes of gold.

"It looks like Ms. Thompson saved our lives. I can't believe that we needed saving so soon again," I said.

I carried the last two loaded pipes, as Rebekah held my arm. We walked slowly back along the river.

"What are we supposed to do with all of this gold?"

I responded, "What do you mean 'we'? It looks to me like this money was your husband's and then was found on your land. It's yours; it's not mine."

She thought for moment as we continued to walk. Finally she said, "Doesn't Kentucky have community property laws? That means whatever income one gets after their wedding is divided equally."

"So you think we're really married?" I asked.

"I certainly do. I most certainly do," she said as she grinned.

As we climbed up to the house site, I thought to myself. I came to this land to disappear, but in almost every way conceivable I had been found. Rebekah turned towards me and we both smiled.

CPSIA information can be obtained at www.ICGtesting.com
Printed in the USA
LVOW12s1002070913

351327LV00002B/4/P